XY

A GOLD Libertarian And

By Russell Hasan

Copyright 2017 Russell Hasan

Contents

Chapter One: Making Money vs. Theft, Fraud, and Force 1
Chapter Two: TANSTAAFL: A GOLD Analysis 18
Chapter Three: An Empirical Refutation of Socialism 23
Chapter Four: Creating Value Causes Private Deflation 29
Chapter Five: Private Deflation Helps the Poor 32
Chapter Six: The Upward Spiral 36
Chapter Seven: Hooey and History 42
Chapter Eight: The Choice Theory of Value 45
Chapter Nine: Windows and Doors Theory 53
Chapter Ten: Economic Efficiency and Outsourcing 58
Chapter Eleven: Who Will Protect Us from Our Protectionism? 62
Chapter Twelve: On Greed 69
Chapter Thirteen: Contract vs. Status 73
Chapter Fourteen: Unions by Force 95
Chapter Fifteen: Freedom of Speech 98
Chapter Sixteen: The Principle of Payment 100
Chapter Seventeen: Private Inefficiencies, Private Corrections 108
Chapter Eighteen: The Freedom to Buy Things vs. the Freedom to Buy Government Favoritism 116
Chapter Nineteen: The Sale 122
Chapter Twenty: The Finite Economy 125
Chapter Twenty One: Work, Luck, Context and Ownership 127
From the Author 137
About the Author 138
Copyright Details 139

Chapter One: Making Money vs. Theft, Fraud, and Force

"He didn't want to *make* money, only to *get* it." –Ayn Rand, "Atlas Shrugged," Part One, Chapter X, page 273 (Signet Paperback Edition).

In my opus of libertarian politics and economics, the nonfiction treatise "Golden Rule Libertarianism" by me (Russell Hasan), I present a bold new theory of economics, which I call GOLD. In the book, I explain the GOLD economics theories of how trade and the money price system are used to coordinate production and consumption in a division of labor economy, and why supply and demand interact with the price system to fine-tune economic efficiency in a capitalist economy. However, after I published the book, I realized that, while I had explained how things work in a good economy, I had not presented extensive detail on what goes wrong in a bad economy. This article will fill that gap.

To begin, I will summarize the GOLD theories of the triangle of trade and the pool of value, which is the core of the GOLD theory. Then I will discuss the difference between making money, which comes from producing a value and trading that value to someone else in return for a value to consume, vs. getting money, which happens when money enters your control without you having produced or traded values, and which is accomplished by theft, fraud, and force. I will proceed by analyzing, one by one, first theft, then fraud, then force. At the conclusion, as an added bonus for you, I will explain what the GOLD analysis tells us about how to make money and get rich.

1. The Triangle of Trade and the Pool of Value.

First I will summarize the theory in a way that can be visualized, and then narratively explain it. XYAB assumes two people, X and A, and assumes that X makes Y, and A makes B. Y and B could be anything, any value, that humans produce and consume in an economy: it could be a pizza that a baker bakes, or a painting that an artist draws, or an hour of labor sewing in a factory to make a dress. It could be anything represented by the abstract variable. There are then two eras, the ancient era, and the modern division of labor era. In the ancient era, X trades Y to A in return for B.

You can:

draw X and A,

write Y with an arrow pointing from X to A,

write B with an arrow pointing from A to X.

Those two simple arrows describe the first era, the simple barter economy of ancient times.

In the modern era, however, trade is a triangle, not a straight line. Here we introduce person C, who makes D. C represents all the third parties in the economy outside of just X and A.

Now draw a triangle.

Label the corners X, A, and C.

Along the outside of the sides of the triangle, label the sides:

Label the XC side as Y.

Label the AC side as D.

Label the AX side as B.

Now, in the middle of the triangle, write "$5".

Look at the triangle. Can you see where I am going with this? To complete the picture, along the sides, draw pointed arrows parallel to the sides, in this way:

Y points from X to C, $5 points from C to X.

D points from C to A, $5 points from A to C.

B points from A to X, $5 points from X to A.

Look at it now. You can see it more clearly by this point:

X makes Y and consumes B,

C makes D and consumes Y,

A makes B and consumes D.

It should look like this:

X's $5 is a sign to A of C's D. X pays for the $5 that he spends to buy B by making Y. X "makes money" by making Y, because Y pays C to pay A for the B that X consumes.

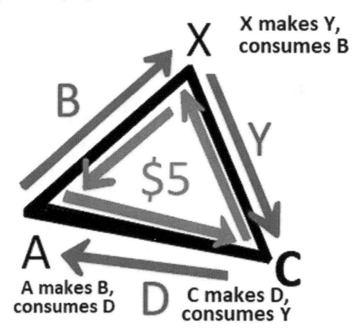

In this way, money, as the representation of value in the economy, is the means for multi-point complex trades of various goods and services among diverse individuals. This is what enables the division of labor economy, where a person specializes in being good at making one narrow type of good or service, in his job or trade or career, then trades that one thing he makes to the rest of the economy, in return for all the various goods and services he wants to consume.

The only things that exist in the economy are the values Y, B, and D, which are traded for each other, with the money as a representation at each trade of the value present at the opposite corner. In a sense, (and I explain this at length in "Golden Rule Libertarianism,") the money is merely a medium of representation, with no intrinsic value: the money's intrinsic worth is merely the paper and ink it is printed on. As such, in the minds of most conventional economists, the money is an illusion that blinds them to what is really happening. But if the money itself is intrinsically worthless, then why does A give B to X in return for a $5 dollar bill?

X's $5 is a sign to A of C's D. When X hands $5 to A, A knows that there is value in the economy that can be bought with the $5, and he knows that, in this economy, a $5 dollar bill is a common medium of exchange, a representation of value. The $5 dollar bill represents $5 worth of value, actual objective intrinsic value, in the economy. This is why A hands B over to X: not because he wants the five dollar bill, merely a piece of paper with ink on it, but because he wants D.

X pays for the $5 he spends to buy B by making Y, because Y pays C to give D to A to compensate A for giving B to X. Thus, when the trade happens on each side, the triangle of trade is complete. Of course, in a modern economy with millions of members, the triangle evolves into what looks more like a circle with millions of segments, or, perhaps, it could even be visualized as a sphere with millions of lines between its different points.

To conclude this summary, when X makes Y, he "makes" the $5 that he hands to A, because Y pays C to hand over D to A for A to consume D, which is what A gets in return for handing B over to X. In this way, my theory explains what it means to "make money."

Now for a far more detailed and less visual narrative. Let us first assume two people, Mr. X and Mr. A. X creates Y, and A creates B. The details don't matter and this is intended to be a broad theory which accordingly would be true if one plugs any set of details into the variables. X's job is to make Y, and A's job is to make B. In a primitive economy 5000 years ago, X and A would live in the same little village, and if X wants to consume B and A wants to consume Y, then they would trade in kind. For example, if X is a blacksmith who makes horseshoes, and A is a farmer who raises cattle, they might trade one cow for a set of horseshoes.

Now jump ahead 5000 years. A modern economy is a division of labor economy, where every person is tightly focused on one particular trade, i.e. his or her career. Assume that X and A live again, and, once again, X makes Y, and A makes B. In a modern economy, Y and B are any value that can be consumed, including a consumable good or service or something that can be used as a tool to make such, and they may or may not be entire products, e.g. they could be tiny parts of a product built by a company, such as a pencil eraser or a car tailpipe. For this example, let us say that X is an auto mechanic in Los Angeles who fixes cars, so Y is auto parts, and A is a baker in New York who bakes cupcakes, so B is baked goods. Let us assume that X wants to order a batch of A's cupcakes over the internet in order to eat them and give some of them to his children. X wants B, and would trade Y for B. However, A does not want Y. Mr. A's care works fine and does not need new parts. The money system is what solves this problem, because money is a common medium of exchange that represents all tradable consumable value. X repairs a car and is paid $40, and X then pays $40 over the internet to A in return for A shipping a batch of chocolate cupcakes to X. A is willing to trade cupcakes for money instead of for a car repair because X's money can be spent by A to buy literally anything else for sale in the economy.

Why is A willing to accept X's money? Here is where the triangle in the "triangle of trade" comes into play. Normally economists look only at the transaction whereby X buys B from A for $40. What they miss, and what nobody pays attention to, is that the trade is a circuit, and the circuit is completed by a tertiary trade, such that the true cycle of trade is a triangle, which includes X, A, and a previously invisible third party, whom I call Dr. C. Generally, X buys B from A for money, A buys D from C for money, and C buys Y from X for money. The money flows in one direction along the triangle and in kind goods and services flow in the other direction. This must be true, because the money has no intrinsic value, but the goods and services are what gets consumed, so ultimately goods and services are what must be traded. In this example, there is a doctor in San Francisco named Dr. C. The engine in his car dies and he buys some car parts for a new motor from X for $40. C also has invented a new medicine for facial acne, called D, and A in New York has purchased a bottle of medicine D from C (i.e. from C's business than sells his medicine) for $40.

The only things that really happened are that X produced Y and consumed B, A produced B and consumed D, and C produced D and consumed Y. In other words, the real economy is a series of in kind trades of goods and services for goods and services, not trades of money, although the money facilitates the trades. The money hides the fact that the only real things in an economy are production, trade, and consumption, and the money merely makes trades possible as a common medium of exchange to represent good and services, without adding anything fundamental to the picture. In a division of labor economy with millions of economic actors, like the USA, the triangle of trade is more like a big circle of trade, with hundreds or thousands of people all trading value in one direction with money flowing back in the other direction.

I say that X's Y "justifies" or "backs" the $40 that X pays to A because the real reason that A gives B to X is not X's $40 that X pays to A. Instead, the real reason that A sells B to X is the D that C gives to A when A pays X's $40 to C. And C gives D to A because X gave Y to C. So, when X makes Y, when X produces Y or does whatever work his job entails that creates Y, when Mr. X creates the consumable tradable value that is Y, X is literally "making" the $40 that he pays to A for B, because he is justifying and backing that money with the value that he produced. This is how the triangle of trade explains the phrase "making money."

When an economy includes, not hundreds of people, nor thousands of people, but literally hundreds of millions of people and billions of trades, then it stops looking like a neat simple triangle or a circle, because there are more than three trades or 100 trades, and instead it looks like a big blob with a billion interconnected trades, which I call a "pool." GOLD economics can be characterized using the pool of value theory, which analyzes this blob using the an extension of the triangle of trade theory. This theory states that when a person works a job, he creates value and puts it into the economy's pool of value and gets money back, and when he buys something he takes value out of the pool and puts money back in. Although I won't provide an illustration, one can envision a circle, with X above the circle, and two lines that connect X to the circle. Along one line, X puts value into the circle and takes money out. For example, getting a salary of $10 for an hour of employment. Along the other line, X puts money into the circle and takes value out. For example, buying a sandwich and coffee for $10. One could just as easily add A and C along the left and right, each with those same two types of lines, one line of putting in value and taking out money, the other line of putting in money and taking out value. To flesh it out further, write an entire alphabet of letters connected to the circle that same way. That circle is the pool of value. The circle gets so big that there comes a point where people, and economists, forget that it is merely an enlarged triangle. But, in fact, X pays for the value that he consumes by means of the value that he produces and puts into the circle.

Under this theory, the total money supply must equal the total pool of value in the economy, because money represents value, so all the money must represent all the value. The pool contains all the goods and services in the economy, and people get money by adding to it, and then spend their money to subtract from it. Thus, to make the money that you get, you must place into the pool of value an amount of value to "back" the money you are taking out, i.e. to make your money.

The pool of value theory explains why printing money causes inflation, because, for example, if there are only 200 dollars in the money supply and only 200 apples in the economy, and the money represents the pool of value, then the value of one apple will be 200/200, i.e. one apple will cost $1. But if 200 new dollars are printed and now 400 dollars corresponds to 200 apples, the value of one apple will be 400/200, so inflation will drive the price of apples from $1 up to $2. Observe that in this scenario, the government has stolen 100 apples, because it can use the newly printed $200 to buy 100 apples out of the economy without having created any value to "back" that newly minted 100 dollars, so the dollar-owning private economy loses 100 apples and those 100 apples are "redistributed". Observe also the logical conclusion of this reasoning that inflation does not help the economy, contrary to Keynesian dogma, because printing money creates more money for people to "get" money, but it does not "make" any money because it adds nothing to the pool of value. By further extension, good economic policy focuses on growing the pool of value, not on growing the money supply, and free trade is the policy that accomplishes this real growth.

I also call the pool of value theory the "correspondence theory of money," because it posits that money corresponds to the pool of value, in much the same way that words correspond to the objects in reality according to the correspondence theory of language. The word "apple" represents any real apple, and a dollar represents any real value that you can buy with it.

Most people do not make something and sell it themselves. Instead, they work as employees and do work for an employer. But, even in this situation, each employee creates a value, which the employer collects, aggregates, and sells to other buyers. The employee sells the value he creates, i.e. his work, to the employer, and the employer trades money, i.e. salary, to the employee in return for that value. The big picture is that the employees all add value to the finished product, and the employer then sells the finished product for money and takes the money and pays each employee a salary for what he contributed to the finished product. So, in reality, each person is trading produced value for money which he will then spend to buy value to consume. Even in the employee-employer model, each employee "justifies" his salary by the work that he does. To frame this using the pool of value theory, when you do work for your employer, you put the value that you create into the pool and get back your money salary, and when you buy things you give your money back and pull value out of the pool.

Subpart 2. Making money vs. getting money.

In her novel "Atlas Shrugged," in Part One Chapter X, there is a sequence of scenes wherein the heroes discover an abandoned factory. For a complicated reason, they seek to learn as much about the factory as possible. They learn that once, the factory was productive and made motors that were sold, but the factory collapsed under owners who did not care about profit. The factory went bankrupt and was sold to a series of crooks who stripped it of its equipment, furniture, etc. The factory was sold to two different people, so its legal status collapsed, and nobody could claim that they owned it, at which point looters broke in and stole everything that was left. During this investigation, over and over again, the heroes talk to idiots who seem to believe that the only way to get money from the factory was to take the objects out of it, like the equipment and furniture, and sell them, or to sell the factory to a sucker. The idea of actually running the factory and making motors to sell, and making money from the factory by creating value and trading it in the economy, does not occur to any of them, although, by implication, it does occur to the heroes.

Rand uses this sequence to point out the difference between making money and getting money. My GOLD theory completes the analysis begun by Rand, by explaining exactly wherein lies the difference. If you seek to make money, then you seek to create a value to trade with others in order to add meaning to the money that you handle. For example, in the triangle of trade example, when X gives $40 to A for B, the value to back up that $40 is the Y that X created and traded to C. Under the pool of value theory, you make money by creating value and placing it into the pool of value to justify the money that you take out. In contrast, getting money without making money consists of pulling value out of the economy without adding any value into the pool of value. In the triangle of trade, getting money breaks the circuit by getting a consumable good or service from someone without having to create value and add it into the triangle through trade with others.

This is almost always accomplished by getting physical money without creating the value to back the money and add meaning to the money. No one is going to feel forced to just give value to someone in return for nothing, but if a thief gets his hands on money, then he can use that money to get value by trading it to other people who see only the money and don't see whether it was made or stolen. The person who created the value consumed by the thief, i.e. the person who takes the thief's money and gives value to the thief, will not know that the money was stolen, and will not be able to see through the complicated web of trades to know that the thief never created any value to deserve to consume what the producer created. The victim of theft, who was robbed, will have been entitled to consume the value that the thief consumes, but this person could be miles away from wherever the thief goes to spend the stolen money.

Unfortunately, in a sense, getting money, as such, includes both making money (where you get the cash you made) and getting money illicitly, by fraud or theft or force. In both scenarios there is a sum of money that a person gets or gets control of. However, to keep our definitions clear and concise, I distinguish "making money", as getting money legitimately by making the value that backs it, from "getting money," by which I mean getting money illegitimately, getting money without making any value that is traded for money to back the money that is obtained.

Subpart 3. Theft, fraud, and force.

Now, having laid our theoretical framework, we can see how theft, fraud, and force work. Theft, fraud and force all consist of getting money and then spending that money without having created anything.

In theft, a thief uses force, e.g. a bank robber with a gun, or deception, e.g. picking someone's pocket, to take money from a person who rightfully owned that money. The thief then spends the money to consume the value that rightfully should have gone to the money's true owner. One of the core teachings of GOLD economics is that the total amount of value that is consumed cannot exceed the total amount of value that is produced, so when someone consumes a value without producing anything, there is necessarily one or more other people who are forced to produce value without consuming the corresponding value they could have traded for. It is in this sense that theft makes the producers into the slaves of the thieves.

Consider again my example of X, A, and C. Now suppose that, after X repairs C's car and gets $40 of payment from C, and thief named Z breaks into X's home and steals $40. Z then buys $40 worth of baked goods from A, and eats them. The production is still the same. Y, B and D get produced. But the consumption is different, because X must now go hungry despite deserving cupcakes, and Z gets to eat when he did not do any productive work. If we could see the network of trades of in kind goods for in kind goods, then A would ship his baked goods to X instead of Z, because he would see the trade of Y to C, which justifies A's sending the cupcakes due to the D that C traded to A. But, because the system of trades is so complex, we only see the money that gets traded. A sees Z's money and A must assume that it is legitimate because he can't see where Z's money came from, so A sends the baked goods to Z, when they should have gone to C. In essence, Z forces X to be Z's slave and work for Z by creating the value for C that makes A give value to Z.

Under the pool of value theory, a thief puts money into the pool and takes out value, but he never put value into the pool to get that money, instead getting the money through evil acts. If replicated on a large scale, this would result in massive consumptions of value with no corresponding productivity or creation of value. Under this scenario, either producers will become slaves, and produce value for the thieves without getting anything in return, or else the producers will stop producing, and the pool of value will shrink.

Now let us consider fraud. Fraud could mean that a person who makes a trade is deceived about what he received on his end of the trade, but I define it more broadly to mean that a person did not get what he wanted. The analysis is similar to the analysis of theft. A sends B to X in return for X's $40, but in reality, it is really in return for C's D that A buys for $40. Now assume that the medicine D does not work, or is not what A wanted, or C lied to A about what D does. Perhaps D makes A's hair turn blue, and does nothing to cure his acne. A created a value worth $40, but A has not gotten to consume the value corresponding to what he produced and traded away. This, again, makes A into a slave, producing value for others to consume while getting nothing in return. C, who defrauded A, gets his $40, and uses it to buy car parts from X. The villain gets money without creating value to justify that money, but in this case, he gets money by fraud instead of by violence as with a thief. According to my theory, if A created $40 worth of value and A does not receive exactly what he chose to buy for $40 in return then A was defrauded by C. In normal situations, this will be identical to A failing to receive the $40 worth of happiness that he paid for (normal meaning that a person chooses to buy the things that will make them happy). This is why, in "Golden Rule Libertarianism," I include a section in the discussion of contract law which focuses on returns policies, because a person should generally be able to void a trade if they did not get what they wanted or did not get what they thought they were getting.

Here let's consider force. As distinct from theft or fraud, which can be done by private individuals, I define force as the systematic distortion of trades in an economy executed by a government using the power of the guns of the police and army to enforce its economic distortions, i.e. the government acts by force. There are two types of force: taxation and regulation. In taxation, the government takes money from private individuals who have earned it, and gives to other people or, as more frequently happens in reality, wastes it on government spending programs that destroy the money without giving anyone what they actually want. As I explain in my book, in a free market economy a trade only happens if two people freely choose it, so the free market economy is what people have chosen. By definition, the economy created by force is different from the free market economy, therefore it follows as a logical necessity that the economy created by force is not what people would have freely chosen, and therefore it is not what people want. By definition, the difference between the economy of force and the free market economy is what the people would not have chosen but which the government chooses for them. This touches upon the basic GOLD theory, which is that, according to the Golden Rule ("treat other people the way you want them to treat you") you should give freedom of choice to everyone else so that everyone else will let you be free to make your own choices. When GOLD is violated, the result is force, because force was used to override the result that would have resulted from freedom.

We can see that taxation is basically the same as theft, in practice. The government takes money from the productive and then spends it. When X creates $40 worth of Y and trades it and (to simplify the example) on that trade $40 is taxes away as income tax and sales tax, then this makes X into a slave, and steals the value that X created. Using the pool of value theory, X puts value into the pool but gets nothing out of it, while the government takes value out of the pool and places nothing into it. In fact, the government is actually taking Y from X and giving nothing to X in return. This fact is obscured by the role that money plays in what happens. The voters see the government taking tax money from X, and this looks less evil and scary than what is really happening, which is that X is a slave of the government, and X works for the government, to the extent that X makes the value that backs the money taken from him as taxes. True communism, where the people work openly for the government as economic slaves, scares mainstream American voters, but the liberal tax and spend politicians use money to hide what is really happening in a tax-based system, which is a degree of communism to the extent that the worker's created value is taken by the government by means of taking as taxes the money backed by that worker's created value.

We can also see that regulation is fundamentally akin to fraud because people don't get what they want and what they paid for. In a free market economy, the trade of Y for B, or of Y for B for D, would naturally happen. A regulation by definition blocks a trade that would have freely happened or directs that one value be traded for something else other than what the traders would have freely chosen. It must be true that regulation by definition distorts the trades that would have been freely chosen because if all freely chosen trades were to happen then the regulations would have no need to exist. Returning to our triangle of trade example, let us say that, in the interests of food safety, a regulator enacts a regulation that bakers in the eastern USA may not ship boxes of cupcakes to buyers in the western USA, lest they go stale while being shipped over a long distance. We have already seen that, in a free market economy, X would buy cupcakes from A. This is the free trade that would complete the circuit of triangle trade, if it were allowed to happen. A has baked the cupcakes, and X would choose to buy them.

But because of this regulation the trade is forbidden to happen. Now, instead, X must keep his $40, and the cupcakes sit idly on the shelf in A's bakery, unsold, until they go stale. In one sense, A's cupcakes have been stolen from X and $40 has been stolen from A, but in another sense, B has been taken from A, to be disposed of as the regulators see fit. The trade is exploded and X and A do not trade value for value, similarly to a fraud, except that with fraud, a sham trade happens, and with regulation, no trade happens at all.

In a trade-based capitalist economy, trade is what connects producers to consumers in a circuit, and it is the prospect of trading to get what you want to consume which motivates the producers to produce. The more regulations and taxes, the fewer the trades that would otherwise have been freely chosen. Thus, regulation and taxation will directly correlate to a decrease in wealth in a free market economy. For example, if $40 of tax money is taken from X, then he is not allowed to take the value out of the pool that he put in, which will kill his motivation to work. Specific to the example of regulation, the trade of B to X for $40 was a key part of the triangle of trades between X, A, and C. Because of the regulation, A doesn't have the $40 to buy medicine from C, so C won't have the $40 to buy car parts from X. The regulation breaks the circuit in the circle of trade and wreaks havoc on the delicate money mechanism that coordinates purchases and sales in a capitalist economy.

Three important differences exist between government force on the one hand and theft and fraud by private criminals on the other hand. First, a person can legally protect himself from criminals, but there is no legal protection from taxation and regulation. Second, when a private thief steals money, he spends it on what he wants to make himself happy. In contrast, when the government spends taxpayer money to help the poor, or for whatever other bizarre reasons are politically in vogue, the money buys things that were not freely chosen by the poor people or other interested parties for whose benefit the money want spent, nor were the purchases chosen by the taxpayers. Instead, the money funds projects chosen by the broken, failing system of bureaucracy and crony politics. So, more often than not, nobody gets anything they wanted while billions of dollars are wasted and everyone ends up poorer.

Third, in a normal capitalist society, theft and fraud will be the exception. On the other hand, in a liberal/socialist society, force will be the norm and free productive trade will be exception. Because force, like theft and fraud, essentially transforms the productive into the slaves of the looters, either productive people will produce as slaves with nothing in return and the value that is produced will be consumed by people who trade nothing to the producers who made it, or, as will more likely happen, the productive people will lose their motive to produce, they will stop producing, and the pool of value will get smaller. Then, with a smaller pool of value, everyone will be poorer, which will prompt the government to stage further inventions (such as printing more money, which will lack any new value to back it), making things worse (e.g. massive inflation), and the economy will collapse into a downward spiral. This is precisely the nightmare scenario fully explored in Rand's economic novel "Atlas Shrugged," and, especially in dark times like the Great Recession, we have the possibility that our fact will mirror her fiction.

Also note that, as the dark times come, people will lose the understanding of the meaning of money, that money represents value and money is made by creating value to trade, because the government will have severed the connection between money and value. Lacking such understanding, more and more people will seek only getting money instead of making money, and the entire populace will fall into a mindset of force, theft, and fraud.

Subpart 4. How to get rich.

It stands to reason, based on the above, that there are two ways to try to get rich: either try to get a lot of money, as by massive Ponzi scheme frauds, or try to make a lot of money, as by being extremely productive and doing a ton of work to create value that other people will really want to buy. The government has a monopoly on legalized "getting" of money, so, unless you have political connections, it is pointless to seek that path to easy money. Some people use quasi-legal ways to "get" money, like cutting corners on quality to save money, charging an expensive price for a low-quality product, giving bad service to the poor while giving better service to the rich, saving money by doing unsafe dangerous things or selling unsafe products that were cheap to make, high pressure sales tactics or deceptive advertising that gets people to buy into deals that they don't want or don't understand, etc. Plenty of people try to get rich by getting money instead of making money, and some of them succeed. But, under the GOLD theory of economics, such a strategy of "getting" money is contrary to the teachings of economics. Instead, the path to riches that is most practical, and also the most noble and ethical, is to try to get rich by making a huge amount of value, and then trading this abundance of value for a lot of money. "Making" money requires making your customers happy, which comes from selling a great product at a reasonable price and giving good customer service. Happy customers mean that you earned your profit, i.e. you made your money.

So, the practical wisdom that flows from this is, if you want to get rich, don't look at the money or think about the money. Instead, think about the work you are doing and the value you are creating. Work as hard as possible, and, even more importantly, maximize the value you create that other people will want to buy. When you create as much value as you can, and then trade as much as possible, then the end result will be the maximum possible amount of money ending up in your hands from selling what you created to other people. This results in having a lot of money, which means that you can buy a lot of consumable goods and enjoy life.

The Randian approach taken by the heroes of "Atlas Shrugged" makes sense here also: come up with a brilliant idea for a product that people will want to buy, like Rearden Metal, or develop a great skill that people will need to pay you for, like managing a railroad track with hundreds of moving parts and dozens of trains every hour without any train crashes. Do this, and you will put yourself in a position to create a vast amount of value, which you can then trade to others for great wealth to get rich.

But, to make money, it's never about the money. It is always only about the value you create and produce, which you profit from when you trade that value to others for them to consume. In other words, you make money by making other people happy. You create value and trade it to others, those other people consume the value you created and it makes them happy, and this "justifies" and "backs" the money your customers pay you, which makes you happy. Making money is a win-win situation, whereas theft, fraud, and force are deadly for their ability to destroy an economy so that everyone loses.

Chapter Two: TANSTAAFL: A GOLD Analysis

Every libertarian is familiar with the term TANSTAAFL, the abbreviation of the sentence "There ain't no such thing as a free lunch," from the bestselling science fiction novel The Moon is a Harsh Mistress, where a group of libertarian radicals overthrow the government of a lunar colony. This idea, that free stuff is an illusion and doesn't really exist, and that when someone tells you they are going to give you something for free it is a scam, is common among libertarians.

Here I will not present the idea as such, but, taking this idea for granted, I will show its justification in GOLD economics. GOLD posits that an economy is merely a group of individual humans, each of whom produces wealth, trades this wealth to other individuals in return for wealth they wish to consume, and consumes this purchased wealth.

The economy, even in a highly advanced country, is fundamentally a barter economy where goods and services are traded for goods and services, but money has developed as a mechanism to make large trades among many different people possible. For example, if I make eyeglasses and you make pizzas, and I want to buy a slice of pizza, you might not need or want my eyeglasses, but there might be a pair of shoes that you want. So, instead of trading you eyeglasses for pizza, I trade you money for pizza, with the guarantee that this money is backed up by a pair of eyeglasses. You might then buy shoes from a shoemaker whose daughter is nearsighted. The shoemaker then buys eyeglasses from me for the money, and money facilitated a trade between three people, each of whom produced, traded, and consumed goods and services–but the money just as easily could have facilitated a trade among 300,000 people instead of just 3, and in today's economy, this describes what happens.

When I make the pair of eyeglasses, I "make money", which means that I create the wealth which is represented and symbolized by the money that I gave you to pay for the slice of pizza. You accepted that money because you can use it to buy any product from any seller for that amount of money, and the sellers will all accept it because it is backed by my eyeglasses that they can be buy with it, and by all wealth in the pool of wealth in the economy that can be purchased by money.

Theft is actually an inaccurate trade: a thief takes money without producing anything and uses the stolen money to buy something, and the seller mistakenly is forced to believe that he is trading that product he sells to the actual producer of the wealth which justifies this money, and not to a thief, because the seller assumes that a person who owns money owns it rightfully. Because each dollar bill is not clearly labeled with the identity of the producer who made that money, i.e. the person who created the wealth that backs that money, it is possible to take money by theft instead of by trade, and to spend it to then get goods and services that rightfully belong to the person who made that money. I will argue that, in some instances, free stuff is like theft, while in other instances, it is like a trade where one person produces wealth but a different person consumes the wealth obtained from trading it.

So, according to GOLD, wealth is created, traded, and consumed. What happens when something is given away for free instead of being traded for something else? There are three possibilities:

1. Someone created wealth and gave it to someone else who consumed it without trading any wealth back to the producer. In this case, it truly is free, in a sense, from the point of view of the consumer, but only because the producer paid for it, and so it was not free for the producer. A gift fits this description, as does charity. In this case, the producer really pays for the wealth that someone else consumes, because the person who made the money decided to give that wealth, in the form they wished to consume it in, to a different person other than themselves.

2. Someone says that something is free, when in reality it has hidden costs that pay for it. For example, when a business provides a free lunch buffet at a presentation of their sales pitch, the lunch is actually being paid for by the money they will make from sales off the people who are drawn in to eat it. If it wasn't ultimately profitable, to pay for the lunch, the sales pitch, and all other costs, the business would not do it. So the "free" lunch is actually paid for by some of the people who eat it, namely, by the ones who are hooked by the sale pitch at the luncheon and buy the product. For the business to say it is free is a lie, and it is a scam and a con game. For another example, on the web there are dozens of dating sites that claim to be "free", and 99% of them are scams where you join for free and then have to pay to fully utilize the site. Generally, if someone offers you something for free, it is too good to be true.

3. It was produced by someone, but has been taken by force and given to someone else to consume. This is like theft, in that the existence of a money economy is used to con and scam the people into not seeing who has created the wealth that is being consumed. When a government says that it is giving something to the people for free, this is inevitably what it means: that someone created wealth, and the government is taking that wealth by force and giving it to someone else for free.

4. There is a more limited category, where people say that something is free, but only because it is paid for in kind with goods and services, not with printed money. For example, in computer programming there is famously a "free software" movement, where software engineers make software and give it away for free to other software engineers. But here, there is actually an invisible trade happening behind the scenes: the computer programmers give free software to the coding community, and at the same time these same coders take other people's free software and use it without paying for it, in a continuous give and take. There is no exact balance where what one gives equals what one takes, but the principle of trade is there. A trade is a trade and what you receive is paid for by what you give, whether it is paid for in money or in some other form of value. For another example, a social club might let members join for free, like a book club or Meetup, but in that case each member pays for

his membership through showing up and participating and being social. In some limited situations, things must be paid for in values other than dollars, and people tend to call such things "free", when in fact they are paid for by non-money wealth.

From this analysis, several principles emerge, most of which I detailed in my book Golden Rule Libertarianism.

First, you cannot consume something that has not been produced, unless someone else produces something and then does not consume it. Wealth, at a given point in time, is finite, although along a line into the future it can grow or shrink. At any point in time, in an economy, a pool of wealth is created, and it is consumed (and, in this sense, being invested is like being consumed in the future). Each unit of wealth was produced by an individual producer in the economy, and is consumed by one. In this finite map of wealth, if one unit of wealth is consumed and there is no creation of wealth to compensate, the pool of wealth is minus one unit, so someone must go without–and this can be either evenly distributed (the taxpayers pay) or the producer can be robbed of the unit of wealth he produced. The government likes to pretend that when it gives things away for free that it created this wealth, as if it grew on trees, but this is obviously impossible. Someone had to create the wealth for people to consume, but, as in theft, people only see the money that pays for what they consume, they don't see the producer who "made" that money by creating wealth, since the producer behind the money is hidden in a money-based complex economy, since no individual can easily be attributed to any particular dollar in a trade with thousands of participants.

Second, if the government gives out enough free stuff, it bankrupts the economy. Each free thing that is given away is actually paid for by the wealth that was created by the people who make money. As we have seen, the created pool of wealth is finite. If more wealth that that amount is given away–and fuzzy accounting, and a divorce between production and consumption, could easily lead a government to try to give wealth away without paying attention to how much wealth is actually there to give–then the economy tries to consume more wealth than was created. If it tries to do this, it consumes all the wealth, there is no more left to consume, and this is how we define bankruptcy. This danger can be hidden early on by consuming the investment capital that the future is relying on, so we consume the wealth that belongs to future generations while leaving our own wealth alone–Social Security debts for future generations, and the massive amount of money the United States federal government has borrowed from the Federal Reserve, essentially borrowing against its own future–is an example. This can hide the threat until it is too late to reverse.

Third, in conclusion, there is no such thing as a free lunch, there is no such thing as stuff that is truly free, because there is no such thing as wealth that was not created by someone–it is a scam to get you to buy stuff, or to vote for someone, or, if it is a sincere genuine gift, it was free for you because the person who gave it to you has paid for it, and it wasn't free for them. People don't see the connections between money and the wealth that backs it, so, in today's capitalist economy, many people, and the government, and even some of the rich, throw money around without really worrying about the value that underlies it. GOLD illustrated the hidden connections between money and value behind the scenes to enable you to see what is really going on.

Chapter Three: An Empirical Refutation of Socialism

Economists are constantly trying to analyze data to find principles. On that note, let us consider the Great Recession. We may debate what caused the Great Recession: Wall Street greed in reselling mortgage-backed securities of subprime mortgages, or government backing for these same subprime mortgages. The issue is debatable, and it all probably contributed. But it is undeniable that the Great Recession ended in December 2014, coinciding with a massive drop in the price of oil and automotive gasoline. The only difference between December 2014 and any other month in the preceding 5 years was the collapse of the price of oil, so we must conclude that this is what ended the Great Recession.

There is no more poignant argument for GOLD economics. What actually happens when the price of an inelastic commodity collapses? According to GOLD, price is the mechanism whereby consumers and producers compare one item relative to all other items, in the context of their supply and demand. American fracking technology released a massive amount of fossil fuels into the marketplace, which nobody had been expecting. At this point the supply of fossil fuels relative to their demand went way up, so the price went way down. When the price collapsed, Americans who would have had to spend $500 on gas for their cars were instead able to spend that $500 on other things, which stimulated the economy enough to end the Recession.

To understand this, let's consider XYAB. Say that X drives to work, and pays oil rigger A $20 for a tank of gas. A sells gas to X. X makes widgets, which X sells to C, also for $20. Now, A suddenly sells gas to X for $10 instead of $20. Next, the amount of money X must pay A for gas goes down, from $20 to $10. The price of gas is inelastic, meaning that its buyers must have it and will therefore pay whatever price is necessary to get it. So this puts an additional $10 in

X's pocket. X can then spend an additional $10, or sell cheaper widgets to C, to compete better against the other widget makers. If X chooses to pay $10 to D for something else, this creates a job for D to make $10 worth of that item, or if X sells cheaper widgets to C, then X sells more widgets, and C then has more money, which he can spend to buy something from D or use to pass on a discount to his buyers, and so on. This continues until A reaches the new price that is the highest price he can charge in the context of the supply of oil.

One of the central principles of GOLD is that the use of money in economics can sometime cloud and obscure what actually happens, as is the case here. If we look at it in terms of trades, and not in actual dollar amounts, it is clear that the people who trade things to the makers of oil in return for oil end up trading less to the oil makers in return for the same amount of oil, at which point these people then have held more of their wealth, which they can then turn around and trade to other people. The increased amount of oil is an increase in the total amount of value in the economy, and, as GOLD theorizes, the value of a dollar is equal to the total value in the economy divided by the number of dollars, so this results in a massive deflation, but what has actually happened is a vast increase in the amount of economic wealth in the economy, and the amount of value that goes to the buyers of oil is equal to the amount of new wealth that increased, as this additional wealth is represented by the difference between the new price of oil and the old price of oil. This is literally the inverse of inflation: when more money is printed and the amount of wealth remains the same, the printing of money causes inflation, whereas, when the amount of money is relatively stable and more wealth is created, it results in deflation. A classic example of the GOLD theory that the value of a dollar equals the amount of wealth divided by the number of dollars, to explain inflation and deflation under the general GOLD theory that money represents value in trades.

So we can see several GOLD economic principles at work: first, that when supply or demand changes the market recalibrates to the new point of equilibrium where a buyer would not pay more to a seller for that product, and, second, and distinctly libertarian in nature, the more wealth people have, the more jobs and wealth it creates, because each new unit of wealth creates a job to buy or sell it or buy and sell what accompanies it, so economic efficiency creates an upward spiral, where having more money creates more jobs, which creates more things, which makes more money, and so on. Sadly, jobs were lost in the oil industry, but the net effect is a benefit to the economy, and to new jobs for displaced oil workers. This is why, also sadly, government taxes and regulations designed to help the poor actually hurt the poor, frequently, because every trade which might have happened but for government regulation would have created new wealth, and each unit of new wealth that is created also creates jobs to go with it, making it or buying it or selling it or making, buying and selling whatever accompanies it.

In this story we can also see a decisive refutation of socialist economics. The socialists would say that the price of gas is dictated by the exploitative greed of the oil makers, and that the surplus benefit of any increased efficiency in oil production would be kept by the oil makers as their profit, instead of being passed on to the consumers, and to the people generally. Certainly, if the oil makers could have kept the price of oil artificially high, they would have done so, as their profit would have grown by billions if not trillions. The fact that fracking increased the supply of fossil fuels which thereby sharply increased economic growth overall shows that the price was set by supply and demand, not by corporate greed, and that the benefits of economic growth naturally flowed out into the economy to be enjoyed by the people, and were not siphoned into exploitative profits by the rich. The facts simply do not support the socialist economic theories of the nature of profits and the setting of prices.

Let's assume that global wealth is $80 trillion, and global population is 8 billion. These are accurate estimates. Let us also assume that socialists take global control and redistribute all wealth to the poor. If all wealth is distributed equally, which we can assume since the socialists believe that 99% of humanity is exploited by the rich 1%, then each person would receive $10,000. In industrial nations, this would be consumed in a matter of weeks to months by each individual. In poor developing nations, $10,000 would be consumed by someone in a matter of months to a year. Then, after one year, all of the wealth in the world would be consumed, therefore, destroyed (remember, XYAB holds that spending money is equivalent to consuming the value which backed that money), but nothing would create any additional wealth to replace it, nor even create wealth as such at all, so the entire world's wealth would be consumed and would run out in under twelve months, and then everyone would die, unless the productive then stepped in and made more wealth. Socialists believe that the rich hoard money to make money scarce, in order to put the poor in a position where they are forced to work jobs they hate, but the data, the math, says that this is a lie. Indeed, if any company was hoarding a treasure chest disproportionate to its expenses, its share value on Wall Street would skyrocket, but the audited financials of all the world's major corporations are looked over by the economists and financial analysts, and this exploitative accumulation of wealth that the socialists posit of the corporations just does not exist, they have hundreds of billions of dollars in revenue and also hundreds of billions of dollars in costs, with profit margins that are in line with their stock price.

    The socialists say that, in the United States and worldwide, the richest 1% own 50% of the wealth, and the richest 10% own 90% of the wealth. This is not what we would expect if wealth is an attribute of work that is done. Human beings do not differ that sharply along averages. But these numbers are deceptive. In the first place, a lot of this is wealth on paper, the number of shares owned by the rich times their stock price, it is not real wealth. A stock certificate is a piece of paper, you cannot eat it. For example, on the list of the 100 richest men in the world, the vast majority of how their "wealth" is calculated is just on paper, the stock they own in the companies they own. In reality, most of the real wealth that goes from corporate America to Wall Street ends up owned by the big mutual funds and pension funds, and their money generally ends up in the hands of the public, in the end, where the wealth is actually consumed.

    Another reason why the 1% number deceives you is a failure to account for proportionality in economies of scale. Assume, under XYAB, that X is an employee of a factory that makes Y, and the factory is owned and managed by the CEO named C. For each Y that X makes, X does 90% of the work, e.g. spends a month assembling it, and C does 10% of the work, e.g. buying the raw materials and factory machines and making the sale to its retail distributor. Assume that Y sells for $10 per one Y, and then assume that the factory, in one month, has one million employees, makes one million Ys, and sells one million Ys, of which X made one Y, because each of the factory's one million employees makes one Y. The mathematical results are clear: $10 million is made on the sale of one million Y's, but X, who does 90% of the work to make his Y, makes $9, which is his 90% share of the $10 Y he made, while C, doing 10% of the work, makes $1 million, which is 10% of all one million Ys that he contributed to making, which sold for $10 million. The one million employees collectively made $9 million, but each individual employee, each X, made only $9, which is the $9 million made divided by the 9 million workers, while C, one real individual human being, actually made $1 million. I think it is actually true that, in reality, rich people usually get rich by achieving an economy of scale, contributing a small amount of creation to the making of a ton of money by running a business where each employee's effort is organized into an extremely productive operation. In most cases, X, by himself, could not make Y, and C was necessary to form the business, manage the factory, buy the raw materials, etc., so the money C makes is as real as X making Y. The math tells us this result is correct, and X and C get the money they made.

    The reason this confuses many people is the math is slightly abstract, and it is hard to conceptualize something in reality that is this big, it is difficult to imagine and picture one million trades in your mind's eye at once, and people don't understand something if they cannot visualize it. Also, X and C, as individuals, each only need one house and one car, but the proportionality of the scale is far bigger for C because C profits from one million sales and X from only one sale, which explains why C's house and car are probably far bigger and more expensive than X's. Again, the math, and XYAB, show this to be the result of economics, not exploitation.

    You might ask: who decides that C's management is worth 10%? The buyer in the act of choosing to buy Y at the price point set by C wherein C gets 10%. If nobody chooses to buy it then that X vs. C allocation is not chosen and C's work is not worth 10%. The Choice Theory of Value says that the market decides. And when C spends his $1 million he is actually consuming some of the value that was made by all the various buyers of Y, one million people, who traded that value to C's company in return for each one Y that each one of those million consumers purchased. This is actually the same value that X consumes when he spends his $9, except he was paid less of it than C because he made far less of the set of one million Ys.

Chapter Four: Creating Value Causes Private Deflation

Here I make a simple yet innovative and powerful observation: that if, according to GOLD, the money supply represents the pool of value in the economy, then, for every marginal increase in the pool of value due to one individual creating one new marginal unit of value, for example a baker bakes a new pizza, then the pool of value increases while the money supply remains at its previous level (assuming that no new money was printed at the same time), therefore there is more value per money, and this constitutes private deflation, the result of which is that each dollar for a dollar owner can now buy more value, with this increase equal to the new value pro rata across every dollar (e.g. the value of that pizza divided by the total number of dollars or, perhaps, of dollar owners). As the ultimate conclusion, productivity which creates new wealth necessarily makes everything cheaper, and this benefit accrues more powerfully to a person based on how poor they are and how few dollars they own, which explains why libertarianism actually benefits the poor the most, next the middle class, and the rich the least, in relative terms, albeit the rich still own the most money when measured in absolute terms.

This post follows up on my last post, in which I explained the economic theory as to why increases in the supply of oil and natural gas due to new fracking technology ended the Great Recession in circa December 2014. A GOLD economic postulate is that the value of a dollar equals the total pool of value in the economy divided by the total number of dollars in the economy. Thus, with newly created wealth (namely, newly created oil and gas) (and by the way, when I say "wealth" I refer to value, not to money) the difference between the old amount of wealth and the new amount of wealth is like a gift given to all dollar owners who buy gas and oil and automotive gasoline. Their dollar now buys more relative to the previous equilibrium between supply and demand. This is why, from a policy point of view, the supply side policies that create new wealth are always better than the demand side policies of taxing and spending, which focuses on wealth redistribution instead of new wealth creation. When new wealth is created, it usually makes prices cheaper, which very obviously inures to the benefit of the poor and lower middle class, since it is in essence giving them a gift. Because the money supply remains constant while the amount of value that backs it increases, there is more value per dollar, which means that, in essence, productive economic activity that creates value actually causes private deflation. So, if the rich actually *make* a ton of money, this inures to the benefit of the poor just as much as the rich, because each dollar bill owned by a poor person now buys more value. A poor person's $20 now buys a full tank of gas for their car, not just one third of a tank, because the rich fracking oil and gas company made billions in the energy industry. This is not a joke nor an abstract theory, this is real life and real joy or real suffering and real death for real people, the lives of the poor and lower middle class, that is at stake in this theory.

In contrast, a policy that makes things more expensive while claiming to help the poor is almost always going to hurt people with scare dollar holdings who just can't afford it, and does not actually create any new wealth to give more to the people than what they had already–hence the naive and ironically self-defeating nature of many liberal platform planks.

Of course, gas won't stay cheap forever, nor would GOLD theory hold such. The decrease in the price of oil relative to other prices will redirect profit-seeking resources away from the production of oil. Thus, in turn, will decrease the supply of oil until oil finds a price where it clears the market, in other words, where its profit justifies the precise amount of resources spent to produce it. This then becomes a new equilibrium point, the price point where supply clears demand, which is the most efficient use of resources in the context of consumer decisions to buy it and the supply of and demand for that commodity, the resources used to create it, and everything else that competes with them. When people choose to buy more, price goes up, which draws in more resources to produce it until it reaches an efficient price, and when supply goes up, price goes down, which takes resources to produce it away until supply goes down to the price that clears the market. Price summarizes and results from an incredibly sophisticated machinery of the economy that measures everything relative to everything else and coordinates the economic behavior of all the disparate individuals in the world– the miracle of Adam Smith's Invisible Hand. This is not complicated, really, it is basic supply and demand from Economics 101, yet both the Keynesians and Austrians frequently just don't get it.

Lastly, while on the topic of the price of oil and supply and demand, this is a perfect opportunity to flay a pet peeve of mine, namely, the theory of marginal utility. The Austrians say that water is cheap despite being vital to humans survival because every unit of water is priced at the value of its lowest use, in other words, for washing your car or something even less important, not for drinking when dehydrated. I think there is no need to say this, since water is valued at the value of the use it is bought for, obviously. Instead, the theory of supply and demand explains it adequately. Water is cheap, despite being a vital necessity, because there is a high supply relative to demand. If there wasn't–and on the Moon and Mars, there won't be–it would be quite expensive. Oil is fundamentally like water, a vital essential commodity, and its recent collapse in price due to supply and demand supports my argument. Why does it matter? Well, why does it ever matter to believe a true theory instead of an incorrect theory? Because, if you apply it, and you are wrong, the results will be worse than applying a theory that is actually true.

Chapter Five: Private Deflation Helps the Poor

It seems counter-intuitive to say that radically free, deregulated, tax-cutting laissez faire capitalism helps the poor, yet this is what I believe–that what the people need is libertarian radicals, not leftist radicals. I have written, in Liberty Magazine, in 2009 (which now seems ages ago), an article why this is so, but, in looking back, the arguments I made, while true, were quite simplistic–employers reward good employees, the poor have the opportunity to climb the social ladder, a strong government can become a dictatorship and oppress the poor even worse, etc. Recently I have come to more sophisticated explanations, using my GOLD theory of economics that I put forward in my book "Golden Rule Libertarianism."

To summarize, the two alternatives, as I see them, are supply side economics, in other words libertarian economics, which is focused on the creation of wealth, in other words, on creating the supply of goods and services, vs. leftist Keynesian and Marxist demand side economics, which is focused on consumption, as if allocation of goods and services to consumers, i.e. the needy, is what matters most. Under demand side economics, what matters to economists is the consumption of goods and services, which will just appear by magic without any need for production, provided that the demand is there, although, in detail, the Marxist believes that government ownership of the factories will solve the production problem, and the Keynesians believe that government spending and control of the money supply will solve the production problem. In both flavors, it is need, in other words, demand, that defines economics, and trade and the creation of value by productive individuals are regarded as a myth or a discredited rumor.

Supply side economics is the policy that lets the productive, the creators, be free to create new wealth. When you get government out of the way, when you leave wealth in the hands of businesses that create wealth instead of taxing it away, when you cut the regulations that block trades in the marketplace from being made, and when you motivate the geniuses of the economy with the potential for vast self-made wealth for the rich who succeed in business, then the productive people, geniuses, hard workers, etc., add to the pool of wealth, creating new wealth that wasn't there before. It's that simple as to why capitalism creates more wealth, while socialism, where there is no reward for productivity, instead it is punished by higher taxes and the wealth you create is taken away from you, does not create added wealth–human psychology is that simple, and humans are motivated by pleasure and reward, not by abstract disembodies ideas of brotherly love that are mere rhetoric and can't be eaten with a knife and fork.

Here is it useful to look at what is, and is not, a zero-sum game. The difference between supply side economics vs. demand side leftist economics, is that according to supply side, wealth is dynamic, the amount of wealth can go up, or down, when new wealth is created or destroyed. You do not take any wealth for granted, and you know you must create all wealth, down to the last dollar, before you can consume it. Contrast leftist Marxist Keynesian economics, where they think the pool of wealth in an economy is static, wealth is automatic (as a result of post-industrial historical forces, according to Marx), the factories and goods and services are just sitting there waiting to be distributed, and if you leave a dollar in the hands of the rich, it must have been taken from the poor, because wealth is a zero sum game, since wealth is not created or destroyed, it is a static pool waiting to be consumed.

GOLD believes that production is dynamic, whereas consumption is a zero-sum game: the amount of wealth changes with more or less creation, but, after having been created, there is a finite amount of wealth to consume, so that, for one person to consume what he did not produce, another person must produce wealth without consuming it. The leftists, in other words, have it backwards.

Now, why does this matter? If wealth is dynamic, then new wealth can be created. According to GOLD, for every unit of new wealth that gets created, which otherwise would not have been creating under a leftist economy, that new wealth benefits the poor, even if the rich created it and own it initially. Why? Here I break ranks with my right-wing libertarian fellows. It does not "trickle down." What benefits the rich does not benefit the poor, there is no reason why it would. I do not care about the rich, nor to help them, nor their interests. They, in general, are doing fine, they don't need our help, and most of them are conservatives who hate libertarianism. No, the new wealth does not "trickle down". Instead, when new wealth is created, the supply of (that type of) wealth goes up. When supply goes up, price goes down, relative to everything else which that wealth can be traded for, in other words, relative to the rest of the economy–including the dollars owned by the working class. So, when new wealth is created, everything becomes that much cheaper–a benefit felt very powerfully by the poor, and which doesn't really help the rich very much at all. When food, clothing, housing, education, become very cheap, with a lot of new wealth created by a libertarian utopia, then the standard of living for all poor people will rise up to lower middle class levels–only libertarianism can win the War on Poverty. Of course, one needs to fully grasp my GOLD theory, the ratio of dollars to wealth in the economy, my theory of the triangle of trade, and the pool of value, etc., and my vision of supply and demand, to understand this fully.

That is why I am a libertarian: because if you let the productive economic forces, which, for good or bad, are often the highly educated rich with access to capital, be free to create, be free of taxes and regulations that get in their way, then when they create new wealth, even motivated as they are by their selfish greed (the true genius of the invisible hand: the more wealth you create, the more money you make, the richer you become, so selfish greed benefits humanity because it is a motivation for productivity, the great motivator, the one that really works), this newly created wealth does, in fact, help the poor, and doesn't even really help the rich very much more than the vast wealth which they had already. If wealth is not just waiting there to be distributed, if wealth is dynamic and cannot be taken for granted and must be created–and is quite difficult to create–then we need a government with policies designed to let people be free to create and trade, instead of a policy focused on consuming the wealth already created, which turns a blind (or malevolent) eye upon the production and trades that made all the goods and services for people to produce.

Chapter Six: The Upward Spiral

In order to explain an idea from GOLD economics that I refer to as the Upwards Spiral, let's consider the example of a sculptor who finds some red clay in a field and molds and bakes it into a clay pot. I use this example a lot in the context of explaining the right to own private property, as it nicely encapsulated the reasons why the sculptor should own her clay pot, and why she deserves to own it even if she did not create the clay nor create the good luck of finding clay, because she made choices and decisions to shape the clay into the clay pot, using her labor to create something that wasn't there before.

However, let's consider it from a different angle here. What is the economic effect upon the economy as a whole of the creation of one new clay pot? In other words, what is the consequence of each additional marginal clay pot? If she hadn't made the pot, then there would just be red clay beneath the dirt in a field. In the absence of the sculptor, there would be nothing. With the sculptor, there is now one additional clay pot. Evidently, she has created new wealth that did not exist before. What does this mean? There is now one new clay pot for someone, say a baker or a family that needs something to store flour in, to buy and use for their uses for a clay pot. They will purchase the clay pot. This then creates a new marginal unit of work for someone to do, say, to be paid by the purchaser to deliver the clay pot from the sculptor's kiln to the house of the family that has bought it. That family then pays the deliveryman a fee for his work. None of these things–the purchase or the job it created or the salary for that job–would have existed in the absence of that one new clay pot. Then, in turn, perhaps the deliveryman takes his fee and buys a sandwich. This then gives a sandwich shop one new sandwich sale which it otherwise would not have had, it spends the money it made from selling that sandwich to buy a marginal additional amount of bread, the baker sells one more loaf and pays more to the farmer who sells him the flour, the farmer has marginally more money to buy seed and fertilizer for growing wheat, and so on.

In light of this example, we can see that each time a producer creates a new value, each time one new unit of wealth is created, it impacts the entire economy beneficially, creating new trades that would not have existed, and each new trade makes money that can pay for more opportunities to create more wealth. This is basically the Broken Window argument in reverse. The Fallacy of the Broken Window says that if you break a window, the money spent to repair it does not help the economy does not have a net benefit, because the net result is everything as it was before minus one window. The Upward Spiral theory says that if someone makes something, the entire economy benefits, in the traditional of Adam Smith, because everything is as it was before but there is now more wealth in the pool of value that is bought by everyone's dollars.

Two conclusions result from this. First, that the key to economic growth is production. The Keynesians, who say that demand causes growth, as if consuming value is the engine of growth, are simply wrong. This should come as no surprise to most libertarians and Objectivists. The family's need for a pot to store things in, their demand, would accomplish nothing if the sculptor did not actually make the clay pot from the clay. In contrast, supply side economics, which focuses on creating conditions favorable to production and the creation of wealth, is the best tool for economic growth. This is not Voodoo Economics, it is in fact basic logic, which sadly most leftists don't care about, since they don't think logically, they think in emotions, and not merely emotions, but negative emotions like envy and resentment. Note that creating more wealth benefits everyone, including the workers and the poor (see my other essays about the Great Recession for details), so supply side economics actually helps the poor. This is not a "trickle down" effect that I am asserting, I am instead asserting that economic growth increases prosperity and the standard of living, which helps lifts every tier of standard of living higher than it was before. Each marginal unit of new wealth created benefits the economy, so the more that is produced, the more trade creates additional opportunities to produce. Thus there is, obviously, the potential for–aptly named–an Upward Spiral.

Second, leftists who might agree with me about the lone female sculptor say that if a factory mass-produces clay pots, and is owned by a greedy capitalist owner, then all the created wealth is taken by the owner and does not benefit the people. Let's consider this. First, the issue of scale. If one million clay pots are produced, then each one benefits the economy, for the same reason that one clay pot would–up to the point where there is unmet need for more clay pots, and once all need is sated, then supply meets demand and the additional creation of new pots is a waste of resources and does not create wealth. So, if a factory creates one million clay pots, they do good, but one million times more than one person could. The miracle of the Industrial Revolution, and the reason we don't live in thatched-roof hovels in pig feces to die from Black Plague or work 18 hours a day for a bowl of gruel, like they did in medieval civilizations before capitalist economic progress and the Enlightenment that gave birth to that progress.

Second, if the factory creates the pots, the newly created wealth belongs to the people, in the sense that its benefit goes to the many people who buy them, the salary for the fleet of employees who now have jobs to deliver them, and to the sculptors, or factory machine workers, who make them, and get paid their salary. Maybe an owner takes a profit. Perhaps the majority of the revenue is the owner's profit, if a profit margin is high. But in the absence of the factory, one million clay pots could not be made, the jobs for delivering millions of clay pots, and salary for those jobs, would not exist, the salary for the factory workers to buy things would not exist, and the world would be the same except minus a vast amount of created wealth. So the owner takes what he deserves, and he gets the money that equals what the marketplace values his work in organizing a successful clay pots factory. You can either have thousands of working class factory workers making a low wage for unskilled fungible labor, or, in the absence of the capitalist owner, these thousands of people would have no job at all, no money, and they and their families would starve. (Of course, the leftists want to believe that the government could take wealth and give it to these people, but again, that wealth ultimately reduces to just a lot of clay pots, or created food, or created wealth, and someone must create it, and some factory must create it to make enough of it to make a difference–the government doesn't create it.)

According to GOLD economic theory, the paradigm of economics a trade where Mr. X creates goods or services Y, Mr. A creates goods or services B, and X trades Y to A in return for A trading B to X, and X then consumes B while A consumes Y. This trade, of one to one bartering of goods for goods, is the foundation upon which the system of money and prices is added to enable trades between three or more different people: A trades B to C for money, A buys Y from X for that same money, X then buys D from C using the money from A, etc. So, in a GOLD analysis of economics, you always follow the values and the trades, you do not "follow the money", in fact you ignore the money and you instead look at what was created, traded, and consumed.

Now let us consider each additional marginal unit of Y that can be created by X. Assume that A wants to use 3 Ys, and A owns 3 Bs. Assume that X has only produced 2 Ys. Now, consider the theoretical possibility that X could produce one more additional Y–a marginal unit of production. Obviously this one additional Y will enable one more trade, or one more unit of trading, to happen–one more Y can be traded for one more B. If X creates the one more Y, up to the limit of A's demand for Y, then one additional unit of trade happens. The result of one additional unit of trade is that A now has one more Y to consume. Assuming that A consumes goods and services to live his life and also consumes goods and services as raw materials to produce the value, the B, that it is A's job to create, this one additional consumable Y for A then contains one additional marginal unit of productive capacity to create B. That one marginal unit of Y that X decided to create then creates a marginal unit of additional B that A will create.

That B, which, for example, C and X want to consume, then creates a chain reaction within the pool of value, within the economy, with more production leading to still more production, which leads to even more production, in an upward spiral that can keep growing and growing. X's choice to invest the blood, sweat and tears to make one more Y, enables A to make one more B, because

A consumes Y to make B, and A's new B might be consumed by C and enable C to make one more D, and so on, and so on.

According to GOLD XYAB theory, demand actually consists of the supply on the other side of the trade, in other words, the demand for the supply of Y is the supply of B, so increased supply will increase demand. The additional Y enables A to make more Bs, so more Bs will be created, hence more trades will happen of Y for B, and each marginal additional trade then gives X more B and A more Y, which increases X's capacity to make more Ys and likewise increases A's capacity to make more B's. Having one more Y enables A to make one more B to trade to X for X to make another Y tomorrow, because, in GOLD terms, the Y that A consumes is the means by which A creates B: part of the consumable value, part of the Y that A consumes, is necessarily the "seed stock" and raw materials and intermediate goods used to in the process of producing consumable end goods, in A's case, to make B, and any truly consumer value of Y that A consumes simply enables A to physically survive or to live a happy life, which then enables A as a worker to produce B.

In other words, part of Y is the means for A to make B, and A buys Y, so X's additional Y will lead to more B, which A will trade to X, who will use that additional B to make more Y, which he will sell to A, who will use it to make still more B, which will then be sold to X, who will make still more Y, and so on in an infinite upward spiral. Just one additional unit of newly created value, just one more Y made by Mr. X that otherwise would never have existed, can have an exponential growth effect in economics. Then, when you add Mr. C to the analysis, and everyone else who trades with X and A, and lots of different newly created values, and lots of trades of value for value, we can have an economic growth effect that is an exponent of exponents.

This is why every increased marginal unit of production, up to the limit of demand for that supply, increase the number of trades that can be made, which leads to economic growth, and makes the economy and everyone in it better off. Hence supply-side economics: maximize production, by libertarian policies that benefit the producers, which gives X the freedom to make more Y, and you maximize the amount of wealth in the economy. This summarizes Upward Spiral Theory, which I also call the principle of marginal productivity.

Chapter Seven: Hooey and History

I have tried to argue, to libertarians, that a truly libertarian federal government in the United States could actually end poverty, completely, if libertarian policies were enacted and a libertarian utopia was created. Not overnight, obviously, but after about 30 to 60 years, which is how long it usually takes for a political sea change to take effect.

The federal budget is about $3 trillion annually, and it seems clear to me that if that budget were cut to $1 trillion/year for military spending and the federal courts only, and $2 trillion worth of value were kept in the economy in the hands of the productive private sector instead of going towards government spending, under the magnification of wealth that comes from increased production (see my chapter on the Upward Spiral Theory), this increased productivity from $2 trillion of capital per year that gets invested into business and otherwise would not have existed but instead would have been spent by the government in waste, might lead to $10 trillion/year of additional wealth in the American economy created over 30 years.

This idea is supported by the common economic theory known as the Time Value of Money Theory: for example (and this has been proven true by economic analysis) if you had invested $1 in the stock market in 1900, your investment could have been worth $1 million in 2000, 100 years later, because invested capital grows exponentially in a typical capitalist economy, so that the monetary value of time is far greater than what common sense would assume. So it is quite plausible and realistic to think that an additional investment of $2 trillion per year today could generate a net surplus of $10 trillion per year in 30 to 60 years, without me even needing to rely on a prediction of technological breakthroughs funded by that investment to lead to vastly increased efficiency to end poverty, such as genetically modified foods that make it much cheaper to feed the hungry, although that too is a plausible argument.

Assume that in 30 years there would otherwise have been 400 million Americans, of whom 200 million would have lived in poverty. This could put an additional $50,000/year in the pocket of every poor person in the country, effectively abolishing poverty. My numbers are estimates, not exact, but you get the general idea.

I have said this and been sharply criticized, insulted, and rebuked, not by liberals and socialists, but by libertarians! The main argument against me is that my theory is "hooey"– simply naive and unbelievable. So let me reply to the skeptics with a lesson about human history.

Let us posit a simple thought experiment. Suppose you took a European person from the year 950 C.E., back when feudal kings ruled their serfs with horses and iron swords. You tell him that, in the future, there will be no kings nor peasants, but something called democracy, and the people will have televisions and refrigerators and washing machines and cars and vaccines, and that humans will set foot on the Moon. He would either not even understand what you were saying, lacking the concepts of cars and vaccines etc. with which to know the meanings of your words, or he would say that this is unrealistic and improbable to such an extreme extent as to be impossible–in other words, he would accuse you of spouting "hooey", and then he would return to tilling his field for his lord or eating his bowl of gruel.

Do you see the point? Ending poverty seems impossible. But what we have today would have looked impossible to someone even 200 years ago, let alone 1000 years ago. The internet and smartphones would have been inconceivable to someone 60 years ago, in 1955. So this idea that I am being naive is itself ignorant of the capacity for historical human progress.

Having established that no reasonable person can rule out the possibility of ending poverty, it simply remains, then, to determine which political policy would achieve it–libertarianism, or socialism?

I would have hoped that among we libertarians, the answer to that question would be obvious. If, sadly, it is not, see my essay about the Upward Spiral Theory, which explain why libertarian policies are capable of achieving literally exponential economic growth. Once a certain amount of new wealth is created, there will be so much wealth that even those who have little will still have a standard of living that to us we would call middle class, just as the American middle class right now has a standard of living that to European peasants in 950 C.E. would have seemed like literally Heaven on Earth.

Chapter Eight: The Choice Theory of Value

    GOLD economics posits the choice theory of value, in contrast to the labor theory of value, which is Marxist, and the subjective theory of value, which is Austrian. I am well aware that many, perhaps most, libertarians are Austrians or are fond of Austrian economics, so I am sure they will be angry for my taking on Austrian theory, and will try to discredit and attack me. I come from the Objectivist-influenced school of libertarianism, which is sharply contrary to the Rothbardian Austrian school, but I believe in one unified big tent libertarianism, and so I want to try to persuade the Austrians that there is some merit in what I have to say. Let me see if I can answer some of their objections, in anticipation. Two obvious objections that I anticipate are, first, that the choice theory of value will collapse into the labor theory of value, and second, that there are factual scenarios which disprove my theory.

    The labor theory of value says that money should be equal to the amount of work done to make the sold goods, in other words, money should equal labor expended. The Austrian theory of value says that value is subjective, in other words, money should equal the subjective feelings of the consumer. The choice theory of value is, perhaps, in between the other two, or, perhaps, is in a different area altogether. The choice theory of value holds that profit is equal to the amount of value that the producer created and added to the raw materials on top of what was there already. Value refers here not only to physical items added to the raw materials, but of work done to improve the raw materials and turn them into a finished product, such work including both physical labor, intellectual work, and making decisions. Assuming that a person has free will, which the choice theory does assume, a person is responsible for their work and choices, hence created the value, hence is entitled to own the profits as their just reward. The choice theory of value, like the Austrian theory, also holds that value begins with the subjective tastes, feelings, and preferences of the consumer, but the point of sale converts this into an objective measurement, where the consumer made a choice to spend $X to buy something, and at this point the subjectivity is converted into an objective value, the mathematical value of $X of the price of the item, which is fundamentally an objective existing thing in reality, which can be measured and compared and quantitatively analyzed, and is not merely a subjective entity in the consumer's mind.

The choice theory of value is so named because it is the choice to buy or sell at a given price which defines the objective value of the product as being objectively worth that price, so that only the freely made choices of consumers in the marketplace can objectively evaluate values. This implies that government bureaucrats could not know objective values in the absence of free market choices by buyers and sellers, so socialists cannot accurately assign productive resources in proportion to the value of the goods they need to produce. The choice theory of value is distinctly libertarian and anti-socialist. The only way to know what people would choose is to give them the freedom to choose and then see what it is that they actually choose. It is not something an economic planner can guess or predict, despite the fact that it is objective and not subjective, hence economic central planning is futile.

According to the labor theory of value, the value of something is defined by the amount of blood, sweat, and tears that went into producing goods and services, hence, obviously, the working class deserves to own everything. The Austrian will say that, if I say that the person who made the value deserves the money, then this collapses into the Marxist position, because doing the work would earn the profit. To which I reply, for an ethical defense of capitalism, we must be able to say that the people who own money deserve to own it, and earned it, otherwise capitalism has no ethical justification for the ownership of private property, and it would simply be random chance that the rich have money, a random chance that would seem unfair and could be fixed in the interests of fairness. Such a moral justification is utterly missing from the Austrian position, when one turns the magnifying glass of critical scrutiny upon the details of Austrian dogma.

The choice theory of value is not the labor theory of value, because the relevant measurement for my theory is the money price that is paid, not the amount of blood, sweat and tears expended to make the product. If a rich person makes a product that people pay a million dollars for, then he made that money, he earned it, and he deserves it and is ethically justified in owning it. My favorite example is the star Major League baseball player, who brings joy to millions of fans and deserves a $20 million/year salary because he brings joy to 20 million people and thereby creates the value to make that money, even though his job is fun and easy compared to the daily grind of a school janitor who makes $10/hour to clean up unpleasant filth. In the market there is a high supply of potential employees relative to a janitor's work, and the janitor's work is low-risk work that does not entail high stakes if he fails in his job, so the value he creates is actually worth $10/hour in the context of supply and demand and the importance of the job. A corporate CEO is like the baseball star, but more so: the CEO of a company that mass-produced products bought by millions of people creates millions of units of value, and he bears the risk of what happens if he fails at his job, which is bankruptcy and disaster for his company, so the value he creates is obviously enough to earn a million dollar a year salary. In a free market society, the people who make lots of money deserve to be rich, and the poorer people who don't make as much value deserve less money, as a conclusion of deductive logic. Profit is not labor, it is value created, which does not perfectly correspond to labor, but the objective measure of value does correspond to money price paid, indeed, it is identical to it.

The Austrian position is anathema to any Objectivist-influenced libertarian, first because we don't believe that subjective things really exist, second because we understand that capitalist economics needs a moral justification for people to believe in its justice or rightness, or it will die. Under the Austrian postulates, that money need not be earned, and that economics exists to prioritize scarce resources, the people with large amounts of unearned money would have their needs and wants held as a higher priority than people who did lots of hard work and created lots of value but have less money, which screams unfairness to any normal human being, although within the narrow, cloistered Austrian community the Austrians probably don't come into contact with average people very often. In the Austrian model there could be people with lots of money who don't ethically deserve to own their money, yet the entire economy would be organized to satisfy their every whim, and this is not fair. My theory solves the problem created by the Austrians: it rejects Marxism while proving that the people who created value have an ethical right to their profits, which includes the profits made by businesses in a capitalist economy.

The choice theory of value is not the labor theory of value, but doing hard work and making smart decisions generally does create value, so you will get what you deserve under GOLD, whereas the Austrian theory is, in the end, value free, and therefore not as good for capitalist politics. The choice theory of value can never collapse into the labor theory of value, because prices don't perfectly correspond to labor, and A is not non-A, price is not labor, so they are two different theories. One won't collapse into another with any greater probability than that Austrian theory will collapse into Marxism, or that Quantum Mechanics will collapse into Flat Earth Theory. If Austrian theory continues to insist that a person does not need to earn money to own money, then they are sabotaging the ethical justification for capitalism, and this may very well lead to Marxism, which, in a sense, means their theory will collapse into Marxism long before mine does.

There are three factual scenarios which will be asserted against me, so let me anticipate them. First, that a man buys a bottle of wine for $200 from someone who walks past him on the street, and in the very next moment he turns around and sells it to someone else who passes by for $400, but he did absolutely nothing to the bottle of wine, hence created no additional value, yet has a $200 profit. Second, that a man makes a grilled cheese sandwich and puts rare, precious caviar into it, but then sells it on a street corner for $5, so its objective worth was not the price that was objectively paid for it. Third, a worker deserves the money they are paid as salary, yet my theory of profit, that it is the value added on top of raw materials and valued objectively by the free market at the price paid for the product minus the cost of the raw materials to make the product, does not account for salary.

In the bottle of wine case, the value that is created is the value of the wine being in the hands of someone who values it for $400 instead of the person who valued it less at only $200. This is value, as the economic theory of arbitrage, well known to Wall Street traders, would understand. The man did the work to create this arbitrage, and the market valued it at $200 of profit. But what if this man did not work to arbitrage it, and found the buyer and the seller by accident? Then no value was created, it would merely good luck, yet a profit was made.

Well, to this I would reply: everything that exists has some degree, big or small, of luck and chance intertwined with it. From the position of the electrons in the atoms that form your cells, to the position of planet Earth relative to the Sun that makes life on Earth possible, to the fact that your ancestors 50,000 years ago lived to reach sexual maturity and procreated, to the prices and details of the things you can buy and sell, to the people you deal with every day, everything is influenced by luck and chance. Thus, when someone creates value, there is always some degree of luck and chance that created it, yet the creator still deserves to own his property as a result of creating it. In other words, luck is everywhere, hence it should not be considered as a controlling element in any specific case as separate from something that hovers around us everywhere and falls out of the analysis. Thus, the presence of luck and chance should not be an argument against a person having done work to deserve something or earn something, since there is some luck in all work that is done. In the bottle of wine case, perhaps 99% of the profit is luck of being there at the right place and time to find that seller and then that buyer, but 1% is making the decision merely to talk to them, buy it, sell it, and hold the bottle of wine without dropping it and spilling it, and we have already evaluated that luck is a non-factor, so this person did create a value that the market priced as being worth $200, therefore he earned $200. In the vast majority of cases, the numbers will be reversed: 80 to 90% of the profit will usually be value created intentionally, and about 10 to 20% of most value is attributable to good luck and chance favoring the productive creator, although in short-term fluctuations luck and chance can play a much greater role, as it does in the bottle of wine scenario, and good luck and bad luck tend to even out to reveal the effect of productive capacity only over a long enough period of time for probability to emerge from randomness.

The thought experiment posits that the man does absolutely nothing to get a $200 profit, but we have seen that this postulate collapses into an impossibility, because the man must have done something to make a sale at all, even if it was just being in the right place at the right time for one split second. The market has valued this minimal amount of work at a $200 profit, so objectively the tiny value he created is actually worth $200 in the evaluation of the market. If the man truly had literally done nothing, and someone handed him $400 and did not get a bottle of wine in return, then this would have been a gift, not a profit. Gifts are not the same as profits in terms of economics, and one does not earn gifts or deserve to own gifts on the basis of the recipient (rather, a gift is rightfully placed because the gift-giver deserved to have the right to give it to a person of their choosing) so the gift scenario would also not be an obstacle to my theory of profit.

Now, for the man who sells caviar in a sandwich for $5, we say that he sold it for less than what it was objectively worth, yet the choice theory of value would say that it must be objectively worth $5, since that it was the marketplace priced it at. Yet why do we say that it was objectively worth more? Because caviar is more expensive than $5. And why do we say that? Because there are people buying and selling jars of caviar for $1000 and $2000 elsewhere. The only reason we say it is objectively more expensive is because there are other trades happening elsewhere in the market where the same product is sold, in money prices, for other amounts. The choice theory of value would say that those other purchases and sales of caviar that price caviar at $2000 are defining the objective value of caviar, and it is on the basis of those objective prices that we can say the man undersold the sandwich relative to its objective value. In the choice theory of value, the objective value of something is priced by the purchases and sales in the market, and the market functions by each individual aggregating to find the price where one unit of a product won't be bought by buyers for more $X and won't be sold by sellers for less than $X because of the supply and demand for it, the price of its competitors, and the price of its raw materials.

In this way, the purchasing decisions of individuals come together to form the wisdom of the market and create an objective evaluation of the value of an item. The individuals decide the price, but Adam Smith's invisible hand guides all individuals into a choreography wherein the sum of all purchases and sales ultimately finds the market price, so one individual who defies the market does not create the price, although the $5 sale does lower the price of caviar ever so slightly below the $2000 it was priced at elsewhere. This Adam Smith invisible hand process is what evaluates an objective value for the product, let us say $2000/jar for caviar. One purchase or sale may define an objective price relative to that one buyer or seller, but the evaluation of the market is what defines an objective price overall. So, yes, in fact, the sandwich was objectively worth more than $5, but it is only true because of those other sales for $2000. If the other jars of caviar were only selling for $5/jar in the caviar stores, then the sandwich might actually be worth the $5 objectively.

We can take the caviar principle and broaden its application. If someone objects that my choice theory of value is incorrect because the amount of profit that is made by selling a specific product is not actually equal to the objective value that the producer created in taking the raw materials and producing the finished product, we can say: why not? Why do you think it is worth more, or less? Often, it will be because elsewhere in the market there are sales which price comparable value differently, but the person who makes this objection is pretending to be blind to that data. If there are no other trades to value the profit, we can answer: no, the market has evaluated the worth of that created value, and has valued it as being worth this amount of money. The market has spoken, so that it the objective worth, and your feelings that it is really worth more, or less, are mere subjective feelings. Specifically, if you make something, and you put a lot of work into it, and you think it is great, but the marketplace rejects it and it sells for a tiny value, or doesn't sell at all and you take a loss, then your subjective valuation is irrelevant, and the product was objectively worth its price in the free market.

The salary objection is simple to answer. I think of work done by an employee as a product made by the employee and sold to his or her employer, from an economist's point of view. Indeed, work is probably the most common product that is ever sold. The raw materials are the factors of production: the employee's food, water, shelter, healthcare, and education. The salary, minus the cost of those factors of production, is the profit the employee makes on selling his labor to his employer. In my triangle of trade theory, an employee sells his labor to his employer and gets the things that he buys as the corresponding value that he receives in return for giving his labor, from other traders who bought the end products produced by the employer, either directly, or, as in the pool of value theory, via an indirect path through many intermediate buyers and sellers. In this sense, it is quite necessary for us to characterize labor as a product sold by the worker to the employer, and my theory of profit and price does account for it.

That exhausts the refutation of these arguments, but I look forward to seeing what other critical arguments will be aimed at me in the future, in the interests of a healthy, open-minded debate and discussion of GOLD vs. Austrianism.

Chapter Nine: Windows and Doors Theory

Everyone has heard the saying "When God closes a door, He opens a window." I summarize an important principle of libertarian political policy with my own spin on this, by saying: "When the government opens a window, it closes a door." The funny thing about doors and windows is that, when you think about it, you can escape to freedom through a door, but not, usually, escape out a window. I call this principle, summarized by the above saying, as Windows and Doors Theory, and it really is central to my politics and economics.

What Windows and Doors Theory states is that, when you consider a political or economic policy, you should consider it as a complete package of every policy that flows from its underlying principle, and you take the bad with the good, and the good with the bad. Three basic principles exist (there may be more, but let's not worry about that here): the libertarian principle, the conservative principle, and the liberal/socialist principle. What Windows and Doors theory really means is that if you have identified something good about one of these principles, your analysis is not complete until you also consider all the bad things about the principle, and, in the end, you should add up everything good and bad and see if there is a net benefit or net disadvantage to choosing that policy.

Let's play with some examples. Assume that there is an epidemic of obesity and diabetes among the poor in the United States. Assume that a politician proposes a tax on soda (or "pop", as they say in the West Coast–I am an East Coast guy, and we call it "soda") and junk food like McDonalds and potato chips. Suppose that experiments are run in cities and towns which adopt this tax, and it is proven that it does, in fact, improve the public health. Is this a good policy?

Windows and Doors theory states that you must look at the underlying principle, and identify the policy as a whole, to evaluate it. This principle here is liberal regulations to manipulate the sale and consumption of food. Assume, in this example, that there is a Midwestern state–let's call it "Iowa", as a purely hypothetical example–which has a politically important role in Presidential primaries, and which has an economy based on the farming of a food product, corn. Let's assume that corn, if paid with taxpayer dollars, can cheaply be processed into high fructose corn syrup, a substance which when added to food makes food extremely prone to cause obesity and diabetes. Let's assume, in this example, that the government is providing vast farm subsidies to the Iowa corn farmers, which results in a huge supply of artificially cheap high fructose corn syrup.

Windows and Doors Theory simply states that you cannot consider the soda tax without also considering the corn subsidy, because they are, in fact, a package deal. In this example, you could have the soda tax and the corn subsidy, so you are helping and hurting obesity at the same time. Or, you could reject the principle, and thereby reject the package of policies that flows from it. In this example, this would look like voting no on the soda tax, voting to end corn subsidies, and then see whether the obesity epidemic is solved by the end of cheap high fructose corn syrup added to virtually every food in the stores. In fact, there is no such thing as the soda tax or the corn subsidy, there is instead one policy, liberal food regulation. But the liberal politicians want you to see only half the story, and see the soda tax while being blind to the corn subsidy, despite it being one and the same principle that underlies them both.

One can see hundreds of different areas where Windows and Doors Theory can be used for political analysis, but I will only go through one final example here, and then let you apply it to other areas yourself. Assume, in this next example, that a poor person is living in a slum. This poor person just recently lost their job, and has no money. Now, let us consider the liberal policy of giving this poor person free healthcare, and government-subsidized low income housing, and welfare money so they can buy food. Let us assume, for the sake of argument, that this poor person will literally die, would starve to death or get deathly sick, absent government welfare. The liberal politician will point to this as the triumph of liberalism, and accuse the libertarians (and conservatives) of issuing a death sentence to this victim, by proposing to cut taxes and slash welfare.

But Windows and Doors Theory says you must look at the fundamental principle and every detail that results from it, to evaluate a policy, and you take the good with the bad, and you take the bad with the good. Let us assume, in this example, that this poor person is fond of cutting hair, and is a talented hair stylist. Let us assume that in his or her state, in order to get a job as a hair dresser you need a hair-dresser's license issued by a state occupational licensing board, which requires taking classes in hair styling, and this poor person is illiterate and can't read and can't afford the classes, and can't even afford the filing fee to apply for the license. Assume that, in the absence of this occupational license regulation, this poor person can, and would, get a job at a hair salon cutting hair, would be very good at this job, would make an okay salary, and could pay for his or her own food, shelter, and medical treatment, without needing any help from the government. So, is welfare and liberal politics really helping this person, or hurting them?

The example can have further details added to this same example. Assume that, in addition to getting a job as a hair stylist, this person would be willing to work as a factory worker in manufacturing. But in this state there is a minimum wage law, and there are laws that mandate a slate of employee benefits that employers must give to employees. The liberals point to this law as a success, saying it helps the poor. But the law has made it so expensive to hire employees, that the companies in the state's manufacturing industry have closed most of their plants in the state, and moved those plants, and those jobs, to Mexico and China, where the wage they must pay is lower, so that it is cheaper to hire employees overseas. Did the liberal policy really help this poor person, or, as a net result of adding up all the pluses and minuses, did it hurt them? In this example, we have conceded that this poor person, right now, will die if welfare benefits for them are cut. Does this mean that liberalism is a good policy for them?

Another interesting thing to consider is that, based on this, a libertarian could concede that abolishing the welfare state might cause great short-term harm to the poor masses dependent upon it, and that the poor might die without it, yet, as a matter of reason and logic, this might not mean that the net result for those poor masses would be bad. In fact, the libertarian could concede the death sentence argument as part of the story yet still argue that libertarianism is ultimately much better for the people than liberalism, because the supposed death sentence that will result from the end of welfare is not really a death sentence after all, since libertarianism will create new jobs so that the people won't need to rely on welfare to survive any longer. Of course, it is the job of the economists to analyze whether the benefits to the people of job growth are greater or lesser than the loss to the people from welfare benefits ending.

Right here I am not going to go through all the hundreds of different policy details that flow from the three central principles of libertarianism, liberalism, and conservatism, and make arguments as to which of the three is actually best. You can probably guess what I would say, anyway. That is not the point. The point is to make you understand the Windows and Doors Theory, which states that, when analyzing a political policy, look first at the underlying principle, then identify every detail in practice which flows from it, and then, to decide whether it is good or bad, consider both the good it does and the harm it causes, and sum up the net result. Just because you can look out an open window, does not mean you should ignore the sound of a door slamming shut. This is a more wise and intelligent method of analysis than what politicians and pundits do right now, namely, looking at some details that are good and turning a blind eye to the associated bad, or blaming some things as bad and refusing to consider other good things that go hand in hand with them. Windows and Doors Theory is the principle of principles-based analysis.

In conclusion, sometimes in order to open a door you must close a window. And sometimes, when you close a window, then a door swings wide open, so that people can actually exit the room through the open door.

Footnote: Do not confuse Windows and Doors Theory with two other theories with similar names, the Fallacy of the Broken Window (in economics), and Broken Windows Theory (in police procedure). They all sound similar but are not related. Also note that Windows and Doors Theory is not precisely identical to the Principle of Unintended Consequences, which states that economists must consider both intended and unintended consequences of a policy. My theory argues that you should look at all policies that flow from a principle as one package and take the bad with the good, which is not quite what Unintended Consequences Theory says, and, also, some of the bad that flows from a principle may, in fact, be intended, as the policy's advocates may not see some intentional consequences as a bad thing at all.

Chapter Ten: Economic Efficiency and Outsourcing

I firmly believe that if a President were to enact protectionist laws to force American companies not to outsource jobs to Mexico or China, as seems to be the trend in the rhetoric from both the Republican and Democratic Presidential candidates, this would constitute theft of money from the Mexicans and the Chinese, and the American government does not have the right to engage is massive theft.

Let me explain why. I will present two examples to make my case. First, consider a scenario where there is a lot of coal that can be cheaply mined and burned for fuel to produce electricity, and it is also possible to build solar panel farms to harvest sunlight for electricity, but that would be much more expensive. Because the coal would be cheaper, the market, through the price system, is telling us that the coal would be more economically efficient than the solar, because the coal is cheaper relative to the solar. Now assume that the working class is forced, by law, to build the solar power plants, instead of mining for coal, to protect them. So, what has happened? If the coal would cost $5 million, and the solar would cost $20 million, the workers are now forced to do additional work to build the solar that they would not otherwise have had to do. What this really means is that $15 million worth of slave labor was forced onto them, in other words, $15 million worth of labor was stolen from them. $15 million is what the market valued the difference between coal and solar at, so this is the price of the amount of work that was needed additionally above what would have been needed for coal to get the solar, and that is the work that was done.

Aha! But, the liberal will say, the cost of medical care for coal miners with Black Lung, pollution harms from coal smoke poisoning the air and water, etc., made it worth it. But here we are toying with the thought experiment. In a libertarian utopia, a person has the right to sue to recover damages if violence is done to him, and poisoning is a type of violence–Rothbard conceded as much, at times. So the cost of medical lawsuits and pollution lawsuits, in a truly free market, would be factored into the $5 million that the marketplace priced the coal at. In other words, in a libertarian utopia all negative externalities are naturally internalized due to the functioning of the free market as well as a functional judicial system that enables legal recovery for harms.

So, no, there truly was $15 million of wealth that could have belonged to the people if they had been able to pay $5 million instead of $20 million for the same amount of electricity, and this was a loss to the people, felt most painfully by the working class and the poor, as the lack of money always is felt by them most poignantly. The law that forced people away from the economically efficient pattern of production that was based on the objectively existing set of available resources represents an amount of wealth stolen from the people who must pay a price over the efficient market price.

GOLD theory holds that money is an illusion and we must always look at the underlying value that the money represents, and ignore the money, to see what is going on. In the coal vs. solar example, there are really three things, coal, sunlight, and a bunch of resources, such as food and water to feed the workers who could mine coal or build solar panels. If the workers mine coal, it is more efficient–faster, for example–so a certain amount of food and water is consumed to do that. But if they build the solar power plant, it is more expensive–say, it takes more work and longer hours–so they must consume more food and water to build the solar power plant. That $15 million that is lost is actually $15 million worth of food and water that is consumed to build the solar plant and would not have been consumed to mine coal for the same amount of electricity as a result. It is this loss of wealth which is the result of economic inefficiency–the destruction of surplus, to use the economist's terminology.

By the way, the purpose of this example is not to debate coal vs. solar. They are hypothetical examples only. I could have said apples vs. oranges to make the same point.

Now, having established our theoretical framework, let's look at outsourcing. Naturally, the American workers would compete with the Mexican workers and the Chinese workers, and the group who did the best work for the cheapest price would get the jobs. But, because of socialist economic policy, the American workers are not allowed to compete. Minimum wage laws prevent them from competing on price, and the various employment benefits that must be given to American workers makes it even more expensive. Factor in currency exchange rates, and the Mexicans and Chinese workers are far cheaper, perhaps charged $6/hour for work that, with all costs accounted for, American workers would demand $35/hour for. The American workers' skill set is not worth an additional $29/hour.

These prices were not necessary, but because of bad laws they are forced into existence. The market, then, must deal with reality as it exists. So, after the bad laws take their effect, the pattern of resources available means that economic efficiency is for the Mexicans and Chinese to get the jobs. If, instead, more laws force the jobs to go to the Americans, then wealth is stolen from the Mexicans and Chinese, who had earned those jobs in fair competition against the Americans, and this wealth will then be stolen from the people who must buy more expensive products, as the sellers seek to recover their added expense relative to the added cost of paying their factory workers, by forcing the consumers to pay more for these products which were more expensive to manufacture. Again, the poor and working class are hit hardest by more expensive products, as well as the working class in China and Mexico, which lack the American welfare system to fall back on.

Obviously the solution to the plight of the American working class anger is to roll back the minimum wage and employment benefits laws, so they can compete in the global labor market and win, but the labor unions won't hear of this, and the workers themselves are not educated enough about economics to see that it is in their long-term rational self-interest to take a lower wage in order to have jobs and avoid the total loss of all salary when their jobs are taken by foreign workers.

In this context, the Chinese and the Mexicans deserve those jobs, and any protectionism is theft, and will wreak havoc upon the delicate balancing act of economic efficiency in the interconnected and complex world of international trade. A trade war of embargoes and tariffs may result, and then access to cheaper resources in foreign countries is blocked, making things still more expensive, and so on. So, the poor, to buy something made in a factory, will pay $35 for something that should cost $6, so that the political parties can get the labor unions to line up votes. I'm sorry, but it's true, and somebody had to say it, and I guess that someone just happens to be me.

Chapter Eleven: Who Will Protect Us from Our Protectionism?

Who will protect us from Trump's protectionist trade policies? Who pays for "Made in America"?

Donald Trump ran on a very specific campaign promise of curtailing free trade and using the threat of tax penalties combined with the promise of tax breaks to pressure American companies to end outsourcing and bring back jobs to the USA from China and Mexico. In my book "Golden Rule Libertarianism," and this book, I have explained a theory of economics that I refer to as GOLD economics. We can use the theory of GOLD economics to analyze Trump's plan and predict what its consequences will be.

I would like to offer certain premises, and then see where they arrive at through a process of deduction, not unlike a geometric proof. I will begin with a definition, and then offer my premises.

Let us define a product, called X, which must be manufactured in a factory. X could be a crate full of chocolate cookies, or a bicycle, or a carton full of bottles of shampoo, or a men's dress suit and pair of pants, it doesn't matter.

Now, my premises:

1. Say that X was made in the USA ten years ago, and it cost the factory $50/hour to pay a factory worker to make X. Say that five years ago the company making X moved the factory to China, where the Chinese factory worker makes $25/hour to make X.

2. Let us assume that it takes a factory worker 10 hours of work to complete X to the point of being ready for sale to consumers.

3. Back when X was made in the USA, the company sold X wholesale to retail stores, which then sold the individual items to consumers, and each X was sold to the retail store for $600.

4. Assume, to simplify for the sake of analysis, that the factory land and machinery and raw materials are trivially cheap, so the only cost of X to consider is the wages of the worker. It cost the company $500 ($50/hour times 10 hours) to make X, and they sold it for $600, making a profit of $100, when X was made in the USA.

But now, today, being made in China, it costs $250 to make X, and the company sets a price of $400 for X, and makes a profit of $150. But the buyer who needs X used to pay $600 for X and now pays $400, so the buyer achieved a net gain of $200 when X was outsourced overseas. Thus, outsourcing led to higher profits and cheaper costs for buyers.

Now, for the conclusion: what happens when President Donald Trump enters the picture? Donald Trump wants X to once again be made in the USA. For this to happen, the American factory worker, who had been out of a job, now once again makes $50/hour, and the factory towns in the Midwest are alive and jumping with new life and energy. A fun and happy day for Americans, right?

But wait: according to GOLD economics, you cannot consume what has not been produced, and for a benefit to legitimately exist, someone has to pay for it. The cost of labor to make one X in China is $250 ($25 times 10 hours), while the cost of labor to make one X in the USA is $500 ($50/hour times 10 hours). The company has to pay an extra $250 per X of wages to the factory workers again. The question then becomes, where does this money come from? That $250 is real, and somebody is going to end up paying it. Who will it be?

This is the conclusion, arrived at by a process of rational deduction, from my premises: there is an invisible man in Trump's plans, not unlike John Galt as the invisible man in "Atlas Shrugged," the man who makes everything possible in the economy without being known or appreciated. Who is going to surrender $250 out of the process of the production and consumption of X, for the worker to make an additional $250, if that $250 worth of additional value is not newly created as a result of Trump's plan?

That $250 could come from raising the retail price of X back up to $600. Then the buyer loses $200 per X. But the retail sellers will pass this on to the consumers as a higher retail price, and these consumers are, ultimately, the same working class people who are getting their jobs back, so they now have jobs, and things are more expensive for them to buy, so there was no net benefit to them, or, at least, the net benefit is greatly different from what the idiots believe it to be.

When prices for shirts and bicycles and cookies go up, this is called inflation, and it can have catastrophic consequences for an economy. There are T-shirts and jeans sold at Old Navy for $20 and made in Asia, which, if made in the USA, would cost the consumer $100. This was the reason American Apparel, a clothes company that famously tried to make clothes in the USA, ran into trouble. When things are made in a country where the cost of labor is higher, the consumer usually ends up paying for it. Beware "Trumpflation", to coin a term, if the consumer ends up paying for the mysterious $250. Trumpflation is Trump-induced inflation where prices soar because everything has become more expensive to make, hence the retailers must jack their retail prices way up to pay for the rising wholesale prices caused by the rising cost of manufacturing. If this all seems complicated, perhaps it is, but reality, and economics, and the truth, really are complicated.

Trump will not want backlash from massive inflation, so let's examine other sources for the extra $250. It could come out of corporate profits, as Bernie Sanders would have liked had this been his plan, which was similar to Trump's, instead of Trump's own plan. Except that, as would often happen in reality, the corporate profits were a marginal part of the hypothetical scenario. The profit in the premises is $150 to $200, which cannot absorb a rising cost of $250, it is just mathematically impossible. Typically, salary as an expense is a greater percentage of a company's budget than is the net profit that it makes, often far greater.

Trump says that the company will bring jobs back because he will give them tax breaks if they bring the jobs back. And, as we are already seeing in practice, he also threatens them with tax penalties to persuade (or bully, to be more precise) the CEOs into bringing the factories back. So let us add this, the "carrot and stick," if you will, into the GOLD analysis. We have not previously considered the taxes paid by the company that makes X, so let's redo our numbers with taxes as a factor.

Say that the federal corporate income tax on the company was 50% of profits, as a net of all the various complicated taxes and fees they had to pay. 50% of $150 was $75, and 50% of $200 is $100. So, if Trump offers a total tax amnesty to get the jobs back, then the company will get back $75, and will keep a full $150 after-tax profit per X, whereas their after-tax profit per X was $100 before.

If this math were real, the company might actually see a net benefit by bringing jobs home. But there are several key assumptions, if this is actually to work. The amount of taxes that the companies were paying, but will now not have to pay, must be greater than the profits the company was making by paying cheaper wages to foreign workers. Call this the Trump Succeeds Condition.

When the comparison in wages is $25/hour to $50/hour, this might work. In reality, to leave behind our little thought experiment and journey into planet Earth, Mexican and Chinese workers often make $6/hour, while workers in less-civilized countries may make even less, while American factory workers, with all the health insurance and other employee benefits that unionized shops extract, can have a net cost to employers of $60/hour, in some factory-based industries with powerful labor unions.

So, unless Trump can give tax forgiveness on the income tax from profits of selling X that is greater than $54 per hour of factory worker labor, there is no way that the Trump Succeeds Condition can be met. Remember, back when we touched upon Bernie Sanders, we observed that the expense of salary wages usually is far bigger a portion of a company's budget than its profits. But if that is true, than taxes on profits will also be far outweighed by the cost of labor.

It is implausible for the Trump Succeeds Condition to be met in most cases, although I am willing to admit that it may turn out to happen more often than I have predicted, and possibly might work on a large scale, if the economy behaves in an unpredictable manner.

If the carrot fails, what of the stick? Well, if Trump imposes tax penalties on the company that makes X, someone must pay for that too, according to GOLD economics. To paraphrase Ayn Rand in "Atlas Shrugged", light is not the absence of darkness, and a threat to take wealth away is not the creation of wealth to pay for something. If a company concedes to this threat of tax penalties, the extra $250 to pay the worker per X still must come from somewhere, and the absence of a tax penalty does not create $250 worth of new wealth to pay for it.

It is arguable that, when there are more jobs in the USA, the American workers who now have jobs will spend more money in the American economy, which will in turn create other jobs to satisfy their needs, such that an infusion of money back into the economy will create growth, and that growth will pay for the extra $250 of cost. That is an interesting idea, and plausible. But it only works if this is not a zero sum game, in this sense: if $250 is taken from the American consumer and given to the American workers as wages, and the American worker then puts that $250 back into the economy, and that is the $250 that is expected to help the economy and rescue the consumer from inflation, then no net benefit would have been created. It would simply be a distribution of $250 from the American consumer to the American worker, and then back to the consumer. If that scenario is a net-net zero, yet prices became more expensive at the rate of $250 per X, then this theory will not work.

The fundamental flaw in Trump's plan, according to GOLD economics, is that it runs contrary to how a free market economy works. If workers in China will work for $6/hour, but workers in the USA demand $60/hour, those price signals tell the company that it is economically efficient to make X in China, so they should do so. X then becomes cheaper, which benefits all consumers, as the consumers' money then goes farther and buys more, more buying and selling stimulates the economy, and this creates new wealth, and (almost) everyone is richer and happier. The American factory worker is the one person in this situation who gets the short end of the stick (although he benefited immensely from buying cheaper consumer goods made abroad). According to GOLD economics, if he wants to compete for the job in a fair competition, he should lower his demands down to $6/hour, or else develops some work ability that he sells to his employer to justify a $60/hour salary.

The elephant in the room that nobody talks about is the labor unions controlling the factory workers and legislating a slate of employee benefits which forces employers to pay the American worker a compensation package of net $60/hour and forbids him from competing for jobs on price, which prices the American worker out of the manufacturing sector in the global economy. Donald Trump won Wisconsin, Michigan, Ohio and Pennsylvania, in the general election, on the strength of stealing Democratic white working class factory worker votes away from the Democratic Party, which combined with his high voter turnout among the core Republican vote in those states to give him the wins, wins which the establishment did not expect. He knows where his bread gets buttered, and he is not in a position where it is politically feasible for him to challenge the labor unions and make America's workers competitive again on a global scale.

Before I conclude, let me briefly reply to my critics who say that the job of making things to sell to Americans "belongs to America" and should therefore be given only to Americans. My reply is that the jobs to make something are created by the people who buy those products that are made, i.e. by the people who have the money to spend to buy the X's made in the factory. I cannot explain this in detail, but refer to the description of the trade between X and A in my book "Golden Rule Libertarianism," where X makes Y, A makes B, and X trades Y to A in return for B, and I show that X's money is fundamentally equivalent to the Y that X makes, and A's job to make B is created by X making the Y. In other words, the job of making what I consume is actually created by me producing what I produce in my job, and the choice of who gets that job to make stuff for me is determined by the choice of where I spend my money that I made to buy the stuff I buy.

A person should be free to do whatever the Hell they want with their money, including paying someone in China or Mexico to make something they want at a price they choose to pay. To say that the jobs of making things for America belongs to America is to say that the money of the American consumer belongs to America, to be regulated as the American government sees fit.

To conclude the GOLD analysis of Trump's plan: the American factory workers are going to get their jobs back, and that is fantastic. Everyone should be cheering for that. But who is going to pay for it?

Update: Now that it appears that Trump intends to pay for "his wall" by a tariff on trade with Mexico, let me articulate that this assumes that the benefit of trade between the US and Mexico is had by Mexico, such that the tariff will redistribute the economic benefit from Mexico to the US, which the US can then spend to pay for the wall. But, according to GOLD, a freely made economic trade benefits both parties. Thus, at least 50% of the tariff will be money stolen from American businesses who trade with Mexico, and, since the cheap Mexican labor makes cheaper things for Americans to buy, the American working class and middle class on a budget will feel this pain the most. Trump's policy is mere protectionism and big government regulation, like any statist leftist, and by eliminating trades that would have happened in a free market economy, Trump reduces economic growth and drags down the Upward Spiral, as I have written about elsewhere. In free trade between the US and Mexico, both sides won, and now, both sides will lose, and the white working class labor union vote who thinks the work will come back from Mexico to them, the winners under protectionism, will instead find that prices will rise so high under Trumpflation, as it is now so much more expensive to make things in the US than in Mexico, that they will suffer a steep net loss, and the American economy will be dragged down. Unless the "Trump Wins Condition" is met, as described above.

Chapter Twelve: On Greed

Ayn Rand used the words "greed" and "selfishness" to describe virtues in her philosophy for its outrageous shock value, knowing that they would get noticed and attract attention if she said that selfishness was a virtue. She made her point, but, in the Post-Randian era, I think that Objectivists should abandon the terms "selfishness" and "greed" and replace them with "rational self-interest" and "the desire to make money", respectively. They don't mean the same thing to ordinary normal people who have never read Rand's books, and, in the common vocabulary, rational self-interest and making money are actually closer to the concepts that Rand was naming with the words greed and selfishness.

Let me discuss selfishness vs. rational self-interest here, and then discuss greed vs. making money later in this essay. Rational self-interest is commonly understood as the quality people would have if they used reason and logic to identify the things that will benefit them over the long-term, whereas selfishness is often thought of as a child stuffing his face with cake, and taking slices of cake away from the other kids, too. If we wish to talk philosophy with other people, we must use words they can understand without first asking them to take a week to read "Atlas Shrugged" as a precondition of knowing what the heck we are talking about. Rand, in Galt's speech and her essays, explained the two definitions of selfishness–the caveman brute pig thug undisciplined glutton, or the smart rational person with values. If we tell people that selfishness is a virtue, and they have not read Rand's books, they will think we are saying that being a pig thug caveman is a virtue, and there is no reason for us to do this.

Some Objectivists revert to the old "selfish" in their own thoughts when they talk about selfish values, without even noticing this in their own beliefs. I have seen Objectivist articles in the

Objectivist media praising certain people, and also praising cultural values, for being selfish, when it actually looks like they are praising someone for being a thug or a pig. This is an easy mistake to make, because Rand's use of the word selfish is contrary to its normal usage, which the human brain would naturally tend to revert to. A switch to the phrase "rational self-interest" would bring greater intellectual clarity–and intellectual clarity is something that no true Objectivist should oppose.

In addition to the smart rational person vs. the caveman thug bully, the distinction between rational self-interest vs. greed also fits nicely into my theory of GOLD economics, particularly my distinction between "making money" vs. "getting money." Making money happens when you create a value and then sell it to people who want to buy it. Getting money is simply every method of acquiring dollar bills without making any money, often through scams and con games or by government interference ("force and fraud," as Rand would say). The problem that arises is that, according to basic Objectivism, making money is good, while getting money is evil, yet the mainstream media, and liberals, the general public, the philosophers, etc., all confuse and conflate the two: they attack getting money as an example of evil greed, and then say that making money is also greedy and is therefore evil. The Randian strategy of reclaiming "greed" as good fails to clear up this Leftist assault, absent a greater clarification as to make money greed being good while get money greed is actually evil even according to the Randian point of view (indeed, I get the terms "make money" and "get money" from a quote from *Atlas Shrugged*, where Rand indicated this.)

Take, for example, two movies: The Hobbit Part Three, and The Empire Strikes Back. Interestingly, when the movie studio licensed the novel "The Hobbit" for a movie, they paid to make one movie based on the novel, but the language in the licensing contract was ambiguous as to whether sequels were permitted, so, even though the actual contractual negotiations were for the sale of the rights to make one movie, and the studio only paid the fee that the seller expected to get for one movie, the movie studio essentially scammed the literary estate of Tolkien that owned the novel, and made three movies out of

The Hobbit when they only paid to make one–hence The Hobbit was made as three movies: Parts One, Two and Three.

Of course, The Hobbit is a short book, so they ran out of the original material halfway through Part Two, and, as a result, Parts Two and Three having nothing to do with Tolkien's original work, and are horrible, badly written, boring, hackneyed dog filth. I mean it. The Hobbit sequel movies are excrement. Part Two is watchable, but Part Three is boring, stupid, and obnoxious.

But the movie studio did it to get money. More money in their pockets was their only motivation. So the liberals would say that this is greed. And it is obviously dirty, yucky, crooked and evil.

Then consider The Empire Strikes Back. Movie sequels are generally all sucky bad crap, never as good as the original. This one was–the original was incredible, but this sequel was just as incredible, magical, shocking, mind-blowing–and then with the "Luke, I am your father," revelation, it achieved Hollywood immortality, and was probably better than the original Star Wars: A New Hope.

But guess what? George Lucas made The Empire Strikes Back in order to make money. Nothing else was his motivation. By all accounts, of biographers and such, George Lucas, as a person, has always cared a lot about money, from his sale of Pixar to Steve Jobs for a huge payout, to his sale of Star Wars to Disney for a huge payout. So an Objectivist would say that *this* is greed. Yet it is beautiful, fun, incredible, and contributed to one of the best artistic achievements in Hollywood's history.

What, then, is greed? Is it making money by creating great value? Or is it getting money through fraud and con games and scams and lies and being crooked and corrupt? I think the word "greed" is so conflicted and abused that we can't redefine it one way or another. To most people, it means the latter, to Objectivists, it means the former. Its meaning is confused. Instead, I prefer the term "rational self-interest," and "the desire to make money," and don't even talk about greed. As for the opposite of rational self-interest, say "irrationality"–it is, after all. If "self-interest" needs a precise opposite, it would be "self-abnegation", the act of destroying oneself, under the Randian analysis. And the opposite of " the desire to make money" is " the desire merely to get money."

And, when discussing things like the movies I mentioned, you can and should actually use the phrases "make money" and "getting money" to identify these different actions, especially from within the context of a GOLD economics analysis, in which the act of making money is actually the act of creating the value that is represented by the dollar bills in your pocket, the value you made and then trades to someone else in return for those dollars, and creating a value is *making* money, literally.

In practice, people say "greed" to mean both making money and getting money. This plays right into the leftists' hands, for anti-capitalist propaganda purposes. The liberals can smear making money, which is good, with the evil of getting money, which actually is evil, and accuse the defenders of making money as being apologists for the get-money scam artists. Then, on the conservative side, as I have written elsewhere, there is a class of the get-money evil rich who are rich because of scams and cons or crony capitalism, and these rich people can pretend to be the good rich, the make-money rich, by aligning all rich people on the side of pro-"greed". The vocabulary is so screwed up that a brand new set of words is called for to bring greater clarify to what we mean when we speak. To paraphrase the famous quote "greed is good," I would say "greed is good at confusing what we mean when we talk about rationality and self-interest and making money and the make-money rich, vs. irrationality and self-abnegation and getting money and the get-money corrupt con artist rich."

Chapter Thirteen: Contract vs. Status

I am going to make a complicated argument in this essay, but let's begin it with some simple thought experiments. Assume that a man devotes 20 years of his life to developing a very difficult and high-paying job skill: for example, in the 1960's and '70's, a man could have spent years developing the skills of mainframe computer maintenance and how to manage hole punch-cards for programming computers.

The man works, studies, makes sacrifices to take job training, spends a lot of money on classes to learn this job skill, relocates to a strange city to pursue better training. Then the personal computer is invented, mainframes die, and the man's job skill is worthless. Can we say that the man has now lost income that he rightfully deserved and was ethically entitled to? If the man is entitled to a certain wage based on his work, should society give this to him to compensate him for the investment in job training, now worthless, which he made? If not, can we at least point to this as an example of where free market capitalism can be fundamentally unfair and unjust due to bad luck?

I offer a second, similar thought experiment. There have been famous lawsuits designed to block affirmative action in university education. Typically, a highly qualified white student with great grades is rejected by a university with an affirmative action policy, where some black students with worse grades were accepted. The white student sues, saying she was denied the place at the university that she had earned from her grades. Does the lawsuit have merit? Should the university be forced to admit the more deserving white student?

Contrary to many of my fellow libertarians, but consistent with the GOLD choice theory of value, I think the answer to all above questions is "no," and the reason is that, in the choice theory of value, the objective value of something is whatever the marketplace values it at in actual trades. Independent of a trade with a buyer and seller who both freely, really, actually, choose to make a trade, products have no objective value, other than in potential. If you have an apple, how much is it worth? When a seller sells an apple for $3, we can say that the apple is worth $3. But absent the sale, its worth is merely a matter of opinion, it is subjective in the Austrian economist's sense until it has an objective price value attached to it. In other words, the market values things, and a thing's true value is what the marketplace says it is. The Austrian says that a thing's value is always subjective, and that money quantities and price are subjective, whereas the GOLD economist says that subjective preferences are translated into objective, quantifiable values through the act of the trade in the free market that assigns an objective money price to something by a person's choice to buy it.

So, in the first thought experiment, the man's skill of maintaining mainframe computers is objectively worth exactly what the market values it as: nothing. It was worth a lot in the '60s and '70s, and after the 1980's it is worth nothing. This is not unfair or unjust, because the man had no right to a highly valuable job skill, he merely did his best to create one, but he failed. Here I will introduce one of the two key concepts in this essay: the sense of "entitlement." To say that this is unfair would be to say that the man was *entitled* to a job because of the work that he did, and that the marketplace should be forced to conform to the efforts of the labor of individuals spent in creating value–which reduces to the labor theory of value, a Marxist theory that I have discussed and rejected elsewhere in my books.

The man was not entitled to anything other than what employers choose to pay him for his job skills, regardless of what work he did to create them. The marketplace now evaluates his job skill to be worthless, so when he failed to get the good high-paying job he trained for, he is getting exactly what he actually deserves, according to GOLD economics and the choice theory of value.

In the context of education and affirmative action in colleges, the same principle applies: the white girl thinks she is *entitled* to the university admission that the school chose to give to the black kid. The trade between two consented traders that evaluates the value of academic credentials is the trade wherein the student "sells" her profile to the school and the school "buys" her as someone desirable by admitting her to the student body. In the absence of a real, free trade between buyer and seller, a product's value is unquantifiable and subjective, and something like that cannot be said to have any value for us to say that it is undervalued or overvalued. If the university values something about a black student more than the white student's grades–such as his life experiences growing up in a poor black neighborhood yet fighting for the chance to go to college–then, in a free market, each party is free to choose any trade for any reason.

The white girl could as easily try to sell an apple to a man for $5, then sue to force him to buy it if he says it isn't worth $5 on the basis that she thinks it really is worth $5 because objectively it is a great, deserving, big shiny red apple that tastes great, which lawsuit would obviously be repulsive to free market advocates and most libertarians. The white girl is free to go to any school that would freely choose to admit her, but there is no objective value to her grades outside of the context of objectively chosen evaluations.

In both cases, we can see that the person pursuing the claim of unfairness, if their position were conceded, would have a massive sense of entitlement, and think they have the moral right to get whatever they feel they deserve. This is the principle of entitlement, which is one of the key concepts I present in this essay. The second, and other, key concept that I need to explain is lower class entitlement vs. upper class entitlement. I will elaborate below, but let us say that the mainframe programmer is from the working class and thinks he is entitled to be provided with a good steady job using hole punch cards to program computers. I call this lower class entitlement, because it is a sense of entitlement to government benefits by a member of the lower class. A member of the welfare class with a sense of entitlement to welfare benefits would be similar. We can contrast this with the white girl who sues to get into college, which is an example of what I call upper class entitlement. Upper class entitlement is when the rich, the highly educated, and members of the upper class, feel a sense of entitlement to their privilege, and then exploit the government for this entitlement to be satisfied in ways that the free market economy does not choose to provide. The white girl is a great example: her rich parents pay for her elite private prep school and tutors, so she gets great grades, and she thinks this gives her the right to force a college to admit her against the college's will. I refer to lower class entitlement as the world of low status, and to upper class entitlement as the world of high status. I view low status and high status to be the same principle, the principle of status, which contrasts to the principle of contract, which I will elaborate upon below.

There is a certain type of rich person who thinks they have the right to be rich, and to live an aristocratic lifestyle, just because they were born into a rich upper class family. Such people are typically white, and they feel they have the right to an Ivy League education because their parents had one, and then, having obtained their Ivy League education, they feel they have the right to get a high-paying job, be rich, drive a luxury car, own a mansion and a yacht, be social among high society, etc. What they have is the belief that they have the right to be rich, and are entitled to be rich, because of their inheritance of status from their family.

The key thing to observe about such rich people is that, from the GOLD point of view, they are completely backwards: GOLD says that if a person creates lots of value and successfully trades it to other consenting traders, then they deserve to get rich from creating and trading value. In contrast, the aristocratic rich believe that they are entitled to succeed in business because they are rich (or, to hear them tell it, because they have impeccable Ivy League credentials which prove they are smart), rather than the GOLD belief, which is that you are entitled to be rich because you have succeeded in business.

The world of high status is mainly that of the heirs who are born rich, but I consider the effects of white racism to be another aspect of the world of high status, one wherein white people think they are entitled to a good job and a certain lifestyle, in a way that other races are not. Just as the rich heir high status creates a culture where the members of the world of high status do favors for each other to maintain their status, so, too, the members of the world of white status create a white culture where the white racists do favors for each other and help each other, to maintain a privileged, entitled class that only they are members of.

Let me clarify that my assertion that many rich people live in the world of high status is an empirical claim, not an analytic claim. Based upon my personal experiences, I have met many rich people, including rich young heirs, who have a mindset and an attitude that they are born into the upper class and as such have the right to be rich for their entire lives, regardless of their individual successes or failures in business. I have met enough such people to make a generalized inference that many rich people share this attitude. I have also encountered white racists, and racism on a scale that supports my theory.

There are libertarians who become rapid and foam at the mouth if anyone criticizes the rich. These people are out of touch with reality, and, since they are wrong, and they refuse to open their eyes and see reality, we can safely ignore them. Observe that most people born into rich families are rich as adults, and most people born into extreme poverty remain in extreme poverty. This is true in the United States and even more so around planet Earth as a whole. To some extent, the rich can pay for a good education, which helps people make money, and there is nothing wrong with a parent spending the money they own to buy what they want, including a better education for their child. But, despite this, if wealth were entirely earned, or lost, through individual effort, for which each individual is responsible, we would not expect to see this heredity in the data, to such a large extent. If the data shows a tendency to a caste system, and the world of contract would not create a caste system, then there is a world of high status that is fighting against the world of contract, as is obvious to people who look at what is happening in the world today. Then, on top of that, economic research indicates that whites tend to make more money than non-whites. Again, absent the deranged lunatic idea that whites are genetically superior, which has been debunked, the logical explanation of the scientific data is the theory of the world of high status, where whites are creating and maintaining an entitled racial class for themselves.

There is nothing necessary about being rich, or white, that makes a person become a conspirator to create an entitled class, and I am not attacking the ability to get rich, nor the existence of rich people as such, nor do I have anything against white people. I have encountered some rich people in the world of contract, who did not have any sense of entitlement and understood that they deserve their wealth because they earned it, and for no other reason. And there are plenty of white people who are not racists and would reject any favors handed to them on the basis of race. However, when a person becomes rich through the world of contact, the fear of future failure, and of becoming poor, may motivate this person to seek to protect his wealth through the world of status. And if a smart person becomes rich, but his kids are stupid, it is natural for him to want to set up a system to give his kids what he has, free from the risk of them losing it–as I will explain later, the motives of the world of high status are paved with gold, while leading to Hell. As such, even if wealth is created in the world of contract, the tendency towards fear tends to corrupt the rich, and whites, into collapsing into the world of high status, out of their fear of losing what they have, and a desire to protect it through ill-gotten entitlements.

The rich would be free to do whatever they want to create an upper class, should they so desire, if they did so within the context of the free market economy. This is never what happens. Instead, for example, Wall St. gets its Obama bailout in 2008, which effectively eliminated the risk for Wall Street investment banks to go bankrupt if they make huge bad bets and lose big. As such, the government has now created Wall Street as an entitled upper class, which cannot go down in status. Similarly, there are real lawsuits like the one by the white girl in my example. The Ivy League, which is a great engine for bestowing high status privilege upon the rich heirs, is effectively propped up by government funding and government jobs that are only available to its graduates. And the government gives favors to rich crony capitalist businessmen, often in return for political fundraising scams, every day. In all of this, the *government* creates the world of high status, so every libertarian should feel good about opposing high status, and it is not an attack against the rich as such, but, rather, against the high status rich.

There is also a certain type of poor person who thinks that, as a human being, they are entitled to food, water, shelter, healthcare, a job, and any material comfort they need in order to survive or be happy, not from doing work and selling their work to anyone, but merely as a result of being human, without having to do any work at all. These people believe in the rights that FDR and New Deal-era socialists developed and that modern socialists have refined, that a human being has the right to "freedom from want, freedom from fear," and so on, which that humans have a *right* to have wealth given to them. This principle reduces to the welfare class, and to low status entitlement, to the sense that you are entitled to take wealth–whom they take it from, they never say, although it is the productive, smart, talented, etc., who end up making the money which is stolen and redistributed. As a practical matter, the entitlement in the world of low status is often delivered through labor unions, who will enable a person to get a job where, in practice, their employer can't fire them, and they become entitled to a suite of salary and benefits for the rest of their lives, as of right from holding a unionized job.

The typical libertarian will point out that, if these people have a right to wealth, then someone must produce it, the producer will then become the slave of the needy, the needy produce nothing and don't make money to buy anything and steal what they don't deserve, etc. Instead of this path, I want to simply point out that, at its core, this type of person asserts entitled to a certain amount of wealth as a result of their status, as a human being (and, almost always, as a member of the working class). Thus, the person who says that humans have a "right to healthcare, a right to food and shelter, etc." are advocating that people should have a massive sense of entitlement, entirely because of their status as human beings (human beings who exist within, and support, a Leftist political context, although the liberals often fail to mention that caveat)–and this is a status that these people were born into and have done nothing to deserve. I argue that lower class entitlements, and the world of low status, is an equal evil to the spoiled brat rich heirs and their world of high status and upper class entitlements–they are both groups who seek to exploit their hereditary status to gain entitlements that their work and choices have not earned.

In a GOLD economic model, a person creates value, and that person sells that value to someone else in return for value that they want to consume, and if they make money in a capitalist economy instead of trading goods for goods in a barter economy, then that money merely represents the value they created and traded, and it buys the value they purchased. I refer to the world where a person gets what they deserve as a result of creating value and then trading that value to other traders in return for what they want from other consenting traders who freely choose to trade with them–in other words, the world where you make money by making and selling value–as the world of contract. Note carefully what I said: "making and selling value," not merely "making value." In the world of contract, it is the trade of what you made that gets you what you want, not merely the making of it.

I refer to the world where you assert an entitlement to wealth as a result of your status, as the world of status. The world of status has two types. The first is the world of high status, where rich heirs, frequently conservative Republicans but also some notable rich liberal Democrats, assert a right to be rich due to their inherited aristocratic status. White racists are the populist version of the world of high status. The second is the world of low status, where the lower class asserts a right to wealth on the basis of their status, under the Marxist belief that the working class has the right to take anything it wants.

The world of status is based on a massive sense of entitlement, where you take everything for granted and argue that it is unfair to you not to force other people to give you what you want, and ultimately it leads away from a market economy, and towards a feudal economy of caste where your status determines your place in life. In contrast, the world of contract lends itself to a fluid, dynamic class system, where your caste is determined by your wealth, which changes and fluctuates based on your success or failure in the marketplace at any given point in time.

There is an old saying, that when feudal royal Europe transitioned to the capitalist Industrial Revolution, modern society went "from status to contract." (The saying originated from a famous quote by Henry Maine in his 1861 book "Ancient Law"). Recent libertarians have described the rise of the welfare state and socialism by saying that Western civilization went "from status to contract, and back to status." (There are five different law review articles published between 1990 and 2010 with this phrase in their title, so the origin of the second phrasing is difficult to trace.) This is, I think, correct. In this essay, I will show that modern society is collapsing into the world of status, from both the far Right (high status) and the far Left (low status), and the world of contract, stemming from America's foundational libertarian principles of the 1700's and 1800's, is disintegrating. In other words, I will argue that the Right embodies the world of high status, while the Left embodies the world of low status, and, in opposition to them both, the libertarians, with our libertarian principles, embody the world of contract.

Examining the competing concepts of American aristocracy vs. European aristocracy helps elucidate this idea. In comparing a European aristocrat to an American aristocrat, circa the 19th or 20th century, we can contrast what the two aristocrats had, where whatever it is that they had come from, and whether it was stable or fluid.

A European aristocrat, historically, had a title, which he was born into, and he could not lose his title (although he could lose his money). In contrast, an American aristocrat, in the past two centuries, joined the American aristocracy by having a vast sum of money, which either he made or which his family created and he inherited. He could lose his money and, thereby, his position. The European-style aristocrat is the world of status, whereas the American-style aristocrat is the world of contract.

The difference between contract and status is not that in status, there is wealth and power and class, and in contract there is none.

No, in the world of contract, there certainly is wealth and power, and inequality, which amounts to a de facto upper class and working class. The real difference between contract and status is that in status you are born into your caste and you are chained to your station in life, whereas in contract your position is the result of your work and your choices and it comes as a result of freely made trades, and your position in society is fluid and can change based on the work you do, for which you take individual personal responsibility. If you compete and succeed you climb up the social status ladder, and if you are stupid and fail you fall down. In contrast, in the world of status, in the ancient feudal world a peasant was chained to his lot of land to farm, and born into the lower class, while the feudal nobleman lord was born into the upper class and entitled to his castle and his title.

It was the Industrial Revolution that unchained the serf and let him leave his lot for a job in a factory, and allowed the rising middle class of merchants, traders and businessmen to amass self-made wealth that let them rise above and surpass the titled noble lords. This was the libertarian revolution of the 1800's, when men went from status to contract.

In modern times, there is a counter-libertarian revolution, of a collapse from contract back into status. The world of high status (conservatives and white racists) want their children to be born into a privileged status (rich, white, male) so that they can be rich in a way that is permanent and free from the danger of loss and poverty– which is a nice thing for a parent to want for their child, and their motives are perhaps that of a loving parent, and not an evil monster– while the world of low status (liberals) want the welfare class (workers, racial minorities and people born into poverty) to be born into a status where they are entitled to a set of government-provided benefits, and the working class are chained to their labor-unionized jobs–again, perhaps their love of the poor and their desire for people to have money and food to eat and not be needy is a nice desire, and they are not necessarily evil monsters.

That having been said, the world of high status is an evil, monstrous world, which collapses back into a feudal system of a ruling class and an exploited ruled class, a world where there is no individual responsibility or personal success, a regimented, controlled world where people are born into castes, and there is no freedom to move. Contrast this with libertarians: we don't care what you were born as, we only care about what you do and what you choose, and we let you be free to succeed or fail. A contract, as I have written elsewhere, represents a *freely* chosen trade, free for both the buyer and the seller. Thus, the world of contract is the only path to economic, political, and social freedom, while the world of status, be it high status or low status, will drag us back to a different era, and wipe out hundreds of years' worth of social progress.

Like a true libertarian, I believe that a rich person deserves to own their wealth–provided that they earned in in freely chosen trades with consenting adults in a free market economy. It is obvious how the Leftist advocates of low status entitlement seek to use the government to create their world of low status. What is less obvious– and the world of high status seeks to disguise it–is that the world of high status also relies on government force. In the feudal era, the lord's status was defended by the knight's sword. In modern times, the high status heirs rely on government regulations to protect their high status from those poor and middle class people who have the natural ability and intelligence to rise up and compete and take market share away from some heirs.

I have chronicled what this government-imposed high status (which is sometimes called "Crony Capitalism") looks like in other essays, and I refer you to my book Golden Rule Libertarianism, where I discuss several examples of this in detail. For example, the occupational licensing regime restricts access to high-paying careers by imposing license requirements that are expensive and which the poor can't afford. Or, for another example, on Wall Street the cost of regulatory and legal compliance is so high that only the rich investment banks can afford to do IPOs. Or, in high school education, the poor kids are funneled into failing public schools which, under the control of the government, have collapsed and which do nothing other than trapping the poor kids into cycles of drugs and crime and lives of poverty–and act for which I blame the government (which owns and operates these schools) and the absence of school choice, although other libertarians blame it on the poor kids not having money to pay for better educations. Then there are the billions of dollars of sheer political corruption and pork barrel spending, where politicians take political donations from the rich in return for giving government deals and state contracts to those same rich people.

I would not object to a world of rich heirs who have their wealth because they, or their parents and ancestors, made that money honorably in a free market, provided that the government and its bribed politicians was not available to prop up their estates–precisely because, in a truly free market, intelligence and ability or lack thereof will reveal itself, and a rich heir in pure capitalism will lose his fortune if he is stupid enough not to have deserved it to begin with, along a time line long enough for good luck and bad luck to even itself out, as it inevitably does in a free market. Somewhat ironically, although fully as my theory would expect, it is often regulations designed to help the poor which in practice buttress the world of high status–for example, the justification for most occupational licenses is to protect the poor from unqualified professionals, when in reality it is a boondoggle for the rich which restricts supply and thereby raises price along the supply-demand curve, which protects no one and prices the poor out of being able to afford quality service altogether. My theory expects this because my theory identifies the world of status, of which high status and low status are two sides of the same coin, and their real enemy is freedom, the world of contract, for which the agents of high status and of low status will unite in order to oppose it.

Let me conclude with some final points. Discrimination against people based on race, gender, sexual orientation, etc., is all designed to create a high status class of straight white people, who can then make more money at the expense of the people who are deprived of those job opportunities–like the white girl, who wants the job opportunities that come from a good college degree for herself, because she is white, so that they will not go to the black student, whom the college had chosen to admit. Thus, in this sense, libertarians should be allied with the Left in the fight against discrimination on the basis of hereditary status.

The world of high status often tries to pretend that it is the world of contract and to disguise high status as contract, to fool and confuse people into thinking that it is ethical and earned, and that high status rich people deserve to be rich. This maps onto the conservative movement seeking to consume and undermine the libertarian movement as a distinct and different political philosophy. Sadly, many libertarians are fooled by this, and they are defending the world of high status because of their actual belief in the ethicality of the world of contract. Unfortunately, both the high status people and the successful people in the world of contract are very rich, so the presence of money cannot be used to distinguish between the two. Many self-made rich people come from the world of contract but then collapse into the world of status to seek to insulate their heirs, who are raised as stupid spoiled brats and would quite easily waste away the family fortune that their hard-working parents created, from the fear of their heirs losing their money in a fluid class society.

In reality, whether a person is in the world of status or contract must be evaluated on an individual basis, with the details of the person taken into account. One clue is that people in the world of contract will only seek to earn their place in the world through contract, but high status people disguised as contract people will talk the language of contract while seeking to exploit high status in their behavior–like the conservative who says he believes in individualism while exhibiting racist behavior, or the conservative rich businessman who talks about tax cuts and economic freedom while taking a huge profit from government favors from his politician friends, to whose election campaigns he made campaign contributions.

Similarly, the world of education is also confusing, in this sense: according to GOLD, good luck in economics is a nonfactor in political analysis, because good luck and bad luck even out over the long term. Thus, inherited good luck is okay, because you make money by the work that you do with the good luck that you are given, and good luck does not translate into making money absent doing hard work, making choices, and being smart. In contrast, inherited caste is not okay, because it collapses into a status system.

So, when a rich child gets to attend an elite private prep school that is a feeder school for the Ivy League, which poor kids cannot afford to attend, is this inherited good luck, which is fine, or an inherited caste system that sets the rich kids into an unchangeable upper caste as separate from the poor kids who are frozen in the lower class, a caste system where only the rich kids have access to opportunity?

Again, this must be evaluated on a case by case basis: if a student must actually think and be smart and work hard to get the good grades, then it is merit-based and okay, but if the system is set up so that a rich person can write a check to get their kid into the feeder school, and this system essentially guarantees the kid a place at Harvard or Yale or Dartmouth, regardless of the academic work they do, and their degree from the Ivy League will guarantee them an above-average job, regardless of whether they have above-average minds or do above-average work, then it is a caste system in which rich kids are entitled to be rich.

President George W. Bush comes to mind, an idiot who are admitted to Yale because of his Senator father, maintained a grade point average of C while at Yale, and who then won the Texas governorship and the White House on the strength of political connections from his rich elitist family and his Yale alumni network. Bush is an example of someone being born into a hereditary aristocracy in America, if ever there was one. (And no, don't tell me that he earned his money, or that he merely had good luck, or that he won office by a fair democratic vote–first, Gore actually won the election, second, Bush lacked any basic intellect or competence that could have maintained his wealth or position in a society of fluid dynamic status, and good luck is not a sufficient explanation for what he had.)

But one can also think of Jeff Bezos, the super-genius behind Amazon, who has created tons of new wealth and economic prosperity by his actions, revolutionizing the realm of e-commerce, redefining books with his Kindle, modernizing the publishing industry, transforming the realm of technology with Amazon Web Services, etc. He belongs to the world of contract, yet founded

Amazon on the strength of the quality of training he had from his Princeton education.

And, to further complicate matters, the same Ivy League schools will often admit the kids who are legitimate geniuses while also admitting stupid rich heirs just because their parents got them into the elite private prep schools, and will give the best educations to both of them, so that they are not entirely high status or contract, and they, again, use the world of contract to hide their world of high status.

So we can see that, in fact, there is no bright line between the world of status and the world of contract, but, rather, a murky, blurry line, which we must closely examine in order to see its boundary accurately. It is possible to evaluate whether we live in a world of status or a world of contract through empirical data: in a world of contract there is high upward and downward social and economic mobility–rich people become poor, poor people rise to the middle class, and middle class people become rich. This is true for individuals but especially for children's class compared to that of their parents, as the IQ and talent of children often differs sharply from their parents, hence they will become richer or poorer than their parents in a society where status derives from the work that one does, in other words, a meritocracy where you get what you earned. In contrast, in a world of status, class is inherited, and there would be low, or no, social mobility. Sadly, in the United States, where are various areas where the data indicates a world of status, although there are also broad areas of data that show the presence of the world of contract in the USA.

We libertarians must seek to fight against the consolidation of society into a status-based caste system, and oppose the world of status, including both high status and low status. Instead, we must fight for the world of contract, where a person is free to create the life that he deserves, and where everyone is a member of the same political class, the class of human individuals in a free democratic republic, in perfect political equality, while at the same time being free to achieve unequal economic positions, in other words economic inequality, in proportion to the different successes and failures that individual human beings achieve, as a result of freely made trades in the world of contract.

While on the subject of the sense of entitlement that many stupid people have, taking for granted that wealth and their means of livelihood will be provided for them, let me be clear that the poor are not *entitled* to the opportunity to get rich and become as rich as the richest for capitalism to be fair–in a fair system, the poor, the rich, and everyone, are not *entitled* to anything, that is the whole point. You might or might not get your chance to get rich, a rich heir might or might not end up bankrupt one day if he mismanages his wealth, there are no stable economic classes, only a dynamic fluid system of individuals making money and taking the results of their actions, good and bad, in the context of the random luck inherent in reality.

People who resent the rich often really resent the rich heirs who stay rich from high status despite their natural stupidity, because this high status is denied to the poor, in *political* inequality–this is precisely what a GOLD policy would destroy, which is why most rich people and most conservatives hate libertarianism. The world of high status knows that the world of contract will destroy it, and the world of low status knows that the world of contract will destroy it, too–hence both conservatives and liberals hate libertarians. It is only the libertarians themselves who seem not to know this, as many of them are confused and believe that the world of contract defends the world of high status, when in fact they are enemies.

Let me conclude by noting that there are two definitions of the word "entitlement": first, that a person is entitled to something if they have a right to it; second, that a person is entitled to something if their title, i.e. their social and political status, gives them a right to it–hence, en*title*ment. Under the first definition, entitlement is fine. A person is entitled to own property, make money, etc., under that definition. It is under the second definition that, as argued above, I say this: that in a perfect world, nobody would have any sort of a sense of entitlement, a person's status would not entitle them to anything, there would be no high status or low status entitlements, and if you wanted to have something, you would have to earn it.

In ancient history, there was only the world of high status. The kings and nobles had status, while the serfs and peasants did not. A turning point came in Europe during the Enlightenment and the Industrial Revolution: for the first time, the poor, the peasants, could become workers, and could define themselves by contract, and achieve a social status based on their work, not their birth. A rising middle class, and merchants who were not nobles yet enjoyed the social status of having wealth, emerged.

A second turning point them came in the 19th Century. In Europe, socialism sprang up. Within the European political structure, a conflict of left vs. right evolved, in which the left was the world of low status (socialism, Communism) and the right was the world of high status, the world of European kings and nobles who never fully went away when capitalism became dominant, and who continued to exert massive political power in France, England, and Germany.

But in the 19th Century, in the United States, and entirely different paradigm developed. Here, too, there was a battle between left and right. Here, too, the left was socialists, Communists, and anarchists. But in America, in the 1800's, perhaps because America had never had kings or nobles before, the right was not the world of high status. Instead, the right was the world of contract, the world of the American rich, who were, of all the rich people in the world, most distinctly those rich people who had made their money, earned their fortunes and deserved to be rich.

As such, in the United States and Europe there was a political conflict called left vs. right. But the European left vs. right was low status vs. high status, while the American left vs. right was low status vs. contract. The 1800's was characterized, in many ways, by rugged individualism, capitalist economic freedom, and the power of the self-made businessmen and merchants, the Vanderbilts, the Rockefellers, the Andrew Carnegies, the JP Morgans. This was distinctly the world of contract, seen in a way which did not, and perhaps could not, exist in the "Old World" where wealth and power were dominated by the nobility who inherited their titles and estates. This world of contract is what was summed up by the phrase "the

Old Right,", and also by the term "Classical Liberal," as some libertarians call themselves.

I posit that in 20th Century America there has been a third turning point, one which is with us even to this day. In the 20th Century, especially in the post-World War II era, the American left vs. right is collapsing into an American version of the European left vs. right. The world of contract is being eroded, undermined, and sabotaged, and the defense of the world of contract on the Right is collapsing (or has already collapsed) into the world of high status, albeit the American version, which is generally based on an inherited title of being white, or being male, or being Christian, although this also ties into inheriting title in the form of inherited "Old Money" family wealth, as the heirs of the 19th Century fortunes view themselves as a titled upper class. The New Right, and, today, the Alt Right, has all but done away with what was once a principled defense of contract, and instead is fighting against the low status left in order to advance the interests of the world of high status, not the world of contract. The American right vs. left has collapsed into the European right vs. left, to the detriment of what was once the distinctly American Right of economic freedom. Ronald Reagan was one last, imperfect gasp of the American Right, but it is now really the European Right under the skin and faded glory of what was once the American Right.

There is nothing wrong with being white, or male, or Christian, the difference is whether these categories, as a social status or title that is inherited, entitles you to some political special treatment which is denied to others, as the ancient lords of feudal Europe bequeathed the divine right to rule to their children, whereas in the old America, children inherited nothing, and found their own way in the world, and made their fortunes, frequently "going West" to find the land of opportunity. That land of opportunity is all but done– although we libertarians are fighting to reclaim it.

I would like to conclude this addendum by going in a slightly different direction, with a new thought. One can think of the difference between contract and status in this way: in the world of contract, the success of one's children is always contingent upon their doing work and making money, and a parent can never guarantee a child's income for life (although, yes, I concede that billion dollar trust funds can come close, but in these, too, the fund can go broke from bad investments and trustee mismanagement, so the heir's position is never perfectly secure and can fail), whereas a noble title does not fail in a high status system, and in the world of status the parent seeks to make their child's success necessary and inevitable.

Characterized in this way, I am willing to say that the world of contract is a reflection of reality, is "pursuant" to reality (see my work on Objectivist ethics in my book "The Apple of Knowledge"), and reflects the way economics works in reality, whereas the world of status is a defiance of reality, and, as such, is an unnatural abomination. In an economy, hard work creates wealth, but the opportunity to do that work always arises from chance, good luck, and risk–be it the risk of the entrepreneur, of the investor who funds him, his trading partners and suppliers, or all of them. And, since there is always risk, a new business in capitalism can always fail. There is no such thing as a necessary success, a success that was not contingent upon factors such as hard work and good luck. Yet the world of status seeks to coopt and bypass economics, and create a moneyed class for its heirs where their success is necessary, without the need for risk, work, or luck to play a role.

Here we can see, also, that the world of high status and low status both share the same worldview of the means of production and of wealth: that it is just sitting there waiting to be taken, to be redistributed to the poor by the left, or to be hoarded and saved for the rich heirs by the right. In contrast, in the libertarian view, wealth is dynamic, not static, it is not just sitting there to be assigned to owners. Instead, in the state of nature, there is nothing, there is no wealth just sitting there, and any wealth that actually exists is the result of an active process of creation, the result of which is that the wealth is owned by the man or woman who creates it.

Owning property without creating it, to us, is evil, is theft, whether it is the theft of the left stealing from the productive rich, or the theft of the world of high status appropriating wealth for its heirs, which, in the end, usually looks like the exploitation of the middle class, and the non-status groups within it, in order to create a more comfortable life for the upper class (think, for example, of the exploitation of middle class blacks and women within firms, who do more work, hence create more wealth, yet receive less pay, than the average comparable white male, according to many research studies).

When I talk about racism and sexism and status, those on the Right may see this as a concession to leftism. This is not true. In pure capitalism, which I advocate, the market corrects if the upper class tries to get money without earning it–the talented black women quits and starts her own firm and out-competes the white men, or, if the rich try to get money on paper without making money, e.g. by inflating a stock market bubble, then the bubble bursts. It is only *government* support, e.g. the Jim Crow laws or the government bailout of Goldman Sachs in 2008, which can create a hereditary upper class insulated from the fluidity and dynamism of the free market, where the natural behavior is the talented people to get richer and the stupid people, be they rich or poor beforehand, to become poorer. The socialism of the left, and the high status of the new right, would both create a caste system with the people on the bottom–except that in leftism, the people at the top are the liberal elite government bureaucrats, and in the new American right, the people at the top are the white men, or the rich white male politicians who purport to represent and speak for the white men. In either system, the people at the bottom are serfs, chained to their station in life, and each person is born into their place in the economy. Not so in capitalism. A hereditary status system, either left or right, is possible only through government control of the economy, because in economic freedom people will naturally go up or down, and exit their lot in life.

The only reason why, to some extent, the modern United States has low social mobility, it because of the government takeover of the educational system, the government-controlled public schools which trap poor kids into cycles of poverty, so that, to be born into a poor area is to be condemned to a bad education and an expectation of a life in the lower class. If rich white kids and poor black kids have different educations, which set them on different paths in life, and if the primary educational system has been taken over by the government in the form of public k-12 education, then the blame for any systemic structural inequality must be laid squarely upon the government, and the differing ability to pay of the parents should be considered an utter non-factor, since the government has taken control, and assumed responsibility, for education of poor children. A private education system would design profitable ways to make money off of poor kids by teaching them skills that would enable them to make more money as adults, so that they could repay bigger payments to their educators, and in cost-effective ways that their parents could afford, because the for-profit educational innovators would make money by doing so, yet the free market is not allowed to operate in the educational realm–but here I go off on a tangent, from which I shall now return.

Today, as in eras throughout American history, some poor kids still do escape and rise to the middle or upper class, and America is not a caste system yet (see, for example, the poor black kids who get rich and famous through American professional sports, as athletes, and which would not exist in the world of white male high status, where such people would be slaves), although it becomes less likely for a poor black kid to get rich with each growing government intrusion into our lives and each new act of government control of society.

It is only natural that every increase in the power of the government should inure primarily to the benefit of the leaders and bosses of that government, and, to the extent that the interests of the people are inimical to the interests of power and the powerful, it is a logical deduction that a bigger government is worse for the public, and that a smaller government and more freedom lets the people be free to live their lives and to go up or down the social ladder. It also follows from logical deduction that the powerful in a democracy will naturally tend to seek power by pretending to speak for and to benefit the people themselves, because the democratic power is vested first in the people, who then delegate it to their rulers. It is natural for the powerful to pretend this because they will naturally seek more power, since, after all, "power tends to corrupt," and so the leaders will have been corrupted, until they are voted out in favor of innocent new leaders who will then later be corrupted themselves, or else until the leaders have figured out a way to collapse the democracy into a dictatorship, and can then consolidate total power into a status-based system. In all of this, ultimately, only libertarianism, civic virtue, and an awareness of what is happening, can protect the people from their leaders and from power's inexorable tendency to corrupt those leaders.

In conclusion, for the accurate and precise examination of politics and economics, it may be best not to think in terms of "left vs. right," but, instead, to think of "contract vs. low status vs. high status," in order to see the real forces that are at work in the political landscape.

Chapter Fourteen: Unions by Force

Libertarians are not "for the working class" or "for the rich." We are not for a specific end. Instead, we focus on the means, and whether they are ethical or unjust. The specific test we have for means is: were the means accomplished through freedom, or by force? And, for us, force usually resolves into government force.

Nowhere is this issue more evident than with labor unions. The Leftists would paint libertarians as being anti-union. Nothing could be farther from the truth, provided that the unions seek to act within a context of political freedom, and not by force. Sadly, many don't, and this is why the Left seeks to pretend that we are anti-union, when what we are is actually anti-force.

In a free market society, people have the freedom to make any deal they want, or walk away, and dictate their own terms, to the extent of their ability. If a group of employees choose to come together, and offer terms to their employer, that they will all get a raise, or else, as a group, they will quit, this is fine, according to textbook libertarian economics. The choice to work a job, or to quit, is a nonviolent, consensual individual decision, so each worker is free to make that choice for himself, and, hence, they are free to choose to quit as a group. If this happens, their employer may be furiously angry, or lose a ton of money, but libertarians would in no way force the workers not to unionize, as is their right in freedom.

But note what I said above: a worker is free to make that choice *for himself*. He may not make it for his coworkers, or use the state to impose his decisions onto his coworkers, under textbook libertarian economic principles. This is basic individualism vs. collectivism. The problem arises when the unions try to use laws to impose their will onto the workers: for example, to force strike-breaking workers not to go back to work, or force all the employees to join the union and pay union dues against their will, or force employers to reach deals with the unions instead of going into the labor market to seek alternatives, or impose minimum wage laws to prevent other non-union workers from competing against the union workers at wages below the union's demand for a pay raise.

All of these things entail the government using force to force people to do things that they do not want to do and would not freely choose to do in a free economy. This use of force, according to libertarians, is evil. Thus, we libertarians are anti-force, not anti-labor union (or, for some of us, not anti-government as such, either). But the labor union left says that we are anti-union, for the mere reason that we believe in individual freedom, as if, by some bizarre insane logic, freedom for an individual person, freedom for a human being to make decisions, is harmful to the interests of labor unions. Of course, it is harmful only to those labor unions who govern *by force*.

We support the right of workers to organize provided they do so without unjust government help, and we would oppose the employer using government force against the employees, just as much as we oppose the labor unions' use of force against employers. The Leftists seek to confuse and muddy the waters by pretending that we are anti-worker, or hate the poor. What we hate is force, coercion, oppression, and control, and what we love, and fight for, is freedom.

In a libertarian utopia, it stands to reason that there will be labor unions, workers and employers will maneuver and scheme to their advantage, there will be pressures and conflicts, but, in the end, the scenario of what ends up happening will be the result of each individual making a choice about what he would do–strike, or work, and at what price–in a climate of economic freedom.

If the collective value of the free unionized workers is sufficient, then the employer will give them a wage that will persuade them to work, and if not, they will strike, or work, or do whatever they choose, and the employer will make his own individual decision about who to hire, and on what terms. A free union worker may get a higher wage, or may end up fired and without a job–a risk he chooses to take, just as an employer, by his decision of whether to grant a pay raise or not, may make more money or go bankrupt, but will bear the individual responsibility for his choice and the result of that choice.

The Leftists who say that they love labor unions, that government laws to help unions are pro-labor, and that the libertarians are the enemies of labor? Those Leftists hate freedom, and they hate libertarians, and smear us, because we advocate freedom.

There have been huge political fights in state after state over whether liberal politicians can pass laws that will force all workers to join unions, even against an individual worker's will. It is typical leftist liberal elitism to think that they should force a worker to unionize against his will, when he does not want to, for his own good, and impose the decision they think he should make, instead of the decision that he has freely made. One could as easily think that a man should be wrapped in chains and forced to dance like a puppet upon one's strings, if one were convinced both that one knows the puppet's interests better than the puppet does, and that this elite arrogant superiority entitles one to forcible control the puppet against the puppet's will. If the worker chooses freely to unionize, this would be his undeniable right, and no true libertarian would get in his way. But the leftists don't only want to enslave the businessmen, they also want to enslave their own base, the working class, which calls into question the extent to which the politically loyal union bosses are actually benefiting their union members, and how many of the union members know it, too.

Chapter Fifteen: Freedom of Speech

Here I am going to make a simple analogy between XYAB economics and freedom of speech. Among legal scholars, freedom of speech is characterized by the theory of the "marketplace of ideas." It is said that we need freedom of speech so that each individual may listen to all of the different opposing points of view and freely choose his beliefs from among the many that are offered.

Freedom of speech is championed by the Left, yet they fail to see the analogy between the marketplace of ideas, and the marketplace itself, the market in economics. XYAB is not merely the triangle of trade. As you would see if you read my book "Golden Rule Libertarianism," XYAB holds that, where X makes Y and A makes B, and Y and B are competing products, the consumer must always be free to choose between Y and B, and to make this decision for himself, and not have the government impose a decision by force. Note that this picture, where Y and B are two competing products, must be kept conceptually distinct from Y and B in the triangle of trade, where they, along with D, form the sides of a triangle.

I will call the Left out on this. They say that, in love and marriage, a person should be free to choose any lover, and to marry whomever they wish. Similarly, in freedom of speech, they say a person should be free to say what they want, believe what they want, and do any political activism they wish. I agree with the social liberals on such issues, as do many libertarians. But why, then, should this freedom end where the marketplace begins? The freedom to choose between competing consumer products, between Y and B, that, too, is freedom. Yet the liberals betray their own commitment to freedom, in the interests of their desire for big government control.

The typical stale old liberal reply to me is that poor people are not free to buy expensive things, so the freedom to buy Y or B is an illusion. I have argued, taking an approach that is popular among libertarian theorists, that this is a wrong belief, because here, everyone has the same *freedom*, rather it is the *power* to buy those things that is missing, because the poor person cannot buy B if he does not make Y, X must make the money to pay for B by making Y, or else X should not be able to buy B, in the triangle of trade.

But, even here, let me continue the freedom of speech argument. If a person is ugly, they cannot get everyone to have sex with them. Then should beautiful attractive people be forced into sex with ugly people? That would certainly follow from the liberal principle that people should be forced to sate the demands of the needs and wants of the masses. Not everyone has the means, or the time, or the intelligence, to listen to every idea in the marketplace of ideas and make a decision about what to believe. Should the government then begin imposing beliefs, to assist the lacking, wanting masses, who lack resources to participate in the marketplace of ideas? Of course, in a controlled society, like a Communist dictatorship, that nightmare really does exist. But the liberals who say they believe in civil liberties, freedom of speech, free love, etc., are hypocrites if they fail to apply that same principle to economic freedom.

Chapter Sixteen: The Principle of Payment

The liberal politicians have a pattern of enacting regulations which violate what I call the principle of payment. The principle of payment simply states that for a thing to exist economically, and to be long-term viable, it must be paid for, which means that the money must be made to pay for it, which really means that someone must produce the goods and services that are consumed in the process of causing that thing to exist.

They especially violate this principle in legislating benefits for the poor. Speaking broadly, liberal politicians tend to enact legislation that mandates a benefit for the poor but then expects the free market and the private sector to pay for it. The free market, however, perhaps using its own lobbyists, is almost never legally required to pay for it, they are merely required to pay for the benefit if it is to be provided to the poor at all. When this happens, this screws over the poor, because the money to pay for the benefit isn't there, and whatever cheaper alternatives the free market might have provided and paid for (and made a profit on, as it is profits which, ultimately, pay for goods to be produced) are legislated out of existence. When this happens, the free market refuses to pay for the benefit and the government does not pay for it so nobody pays for it, it never exists, and the poor are left with nothing.

I have several examples to show you to elaborate on this.

1. Take, for example, net neutrality. The liberals say that the big Silicon Valley corporations should not be allowed to provide free or cheap internet access to their own websites and apps but not to their competitors, because it will put the Web under their control and is unfair to the other smaller websites. But the advocates of net neutrality are not at the same time going to legislate that free or cheap internet access to every website be provided to the poor at the

government's expense. So, as a result, if the net neutrality advocates win, the poor lose their free or cheaper internet access to the big websites and apps, and nobody pays for them to have internet access, and nobody gives a damn about them, but the liberals get to feel proudly self-righteous and pretend that they helped the poor.

2. For another example, minimum wage laws. The liberals mandate that every job must pay a living wage. There's just one problem: they do not at the same time mandate that every person must be given a job. And if they did, the economy and society would very quickly realize that the money to pay for that isn't there. When a business has a finite amount of revenue coming in, and the cost per job goes up above what they would freely pay, the net result is the number of jobs that the business can afford goes down, and jobs are destroyed or else new jobs that would have existed can't exist.

This is basic math. If a business pays each of five workers $30,000 per year, a total of $150,000, and it has a revenue that allows a budget of $150,000 for salary, and the minimum wage goes up and it now costs $50,000 per year per employee, then the business can only afford to have three employees, $150,000 divided by $50,000 equals three. There is no way to change this result by magic or wishful thinking. The liberals assume that the business will keep its five workers because it "has to," and will just pay them more salary out of corporate profits. But, in the first place, the businesses won't and don't, and, in the second place, profit margins are generally only around five percent to thirty percent, with most hovering around ten percent, so most businesses couldn't even if they wanted to.

As a result of this absurd liberal paternalism, the poor are denied low-paying jobs, and instead some of them who could have had jobs, or did have jobs, get no jobs at all, although the smaller number of poor people who are lucky enough to have a job now make more money. Then, if the free market is allowed to shift jobs to overseas labor forces with far lower minimum wages, vast numbers of the poor get screwed over by being priced out of competing in the labor market for jobs.

3. Occupational licensing. Attorneys cannot practice law unless licensed, and cannot get a license until they graduate law school and pass the bar exam. As a result, the attorneys who can represent clients are good, smart, competent lawyers. A bad lawyer has the power to screw over his clients, and the vulnerable poor are protected from this. I do not deny that. There's just one problem: the law does not, at the same time, pay for poor people to have access to lawyers. Going to law school and sitting for the bar exam is expensive, and lawyers must charge higher legal fees to pay for them, to say nothing of the fact that restricting the supply of attorneys must raise price along the supply and demand curves of economics. So the poor are priced out of being able to afford a lawyer altogether, by these laws, although the ones who can afford a lawyer get a better lawyer. The same is true of doctors and medical school and medical licenses, as well as the dozens of other professions for which state-controlled licensing schemes are popping up.

4. Laws forbid poor people from getting jobs as prostitutes or drug dealers, ostensibly to protect the communities where these sinful behaviors would exist, especially poor and black and Hispanic neighborhoods. The problem is, again, that these laws outlaw the few very high-paying jobs that the poor had access to, all in the name of protecting the poor, yet the law does not then provide alternative high-paying jobs for the poor. The net result is that the poor lose out on the few high paying jobs they actually could have gotten.

5. College tuition. The government is in the practice of giving student loans, or using public backing for private student loans. In a student loan made privately in the free market, the student takes the loan, the loan pays for the student's education, the education teaches job skills that enable the adult to make a lot more money than he otherwise would have, and this additional money then pays back the loan, with interest. But with public loans, which the free market never would have offered at those interest rates, there is no connection between the loan and the job skills, so loans are being given to fund educations that don't pay for the cost with better job skills, and, simultaneously, a total divorce between the costs of

education and the benefits of education is developing, since the colleges can charge whatever they want for worthless garbage and the lenders will pay for it. With government interference in the arena of loans, the government has reaches a new low: instead of giving the poor a benefit and the government paying for it, or mandating a benefit which no one pays for, the government is inciting the poor to receive a benefit they can't afford to pay for, and then setting the poor up to have to pay for it themselves. The student debt is owned by the student, not by the government nor the free market. So we have the rising problem of a generation of young people who were not rich enough to afford college, got a degree that doesn't pay for its own costs, and is now saddled with crippling student loan debt.

The government is essentially letting poor buy something on credit which the poor can't really afford on their income, which would be a predatory practice that could be criminally prosecuted under consumer protection laws, if a private business did it, but which is somehow noble and generous when the government does it to poor students for college educations.

XYAB economics would be quick to point out that the real cost of an education is the value consumed by the university in providing that education to a student: books to buy for the library, buildings to maintain, professors who need food to eat, educational materials to obtain, the food and buildings for the students themselves, etc. If this value is consumed, then someone is going to really pay for that education, it cannot be paid for with fake Monopoly money. The government isn't paying for it (and there isn't enough wealth in the world to actually pay for college education for every kid in the world), and the free market doesn't pay for it. So, the value really is consumed, and the student really does have a death trap wrapped around his neck when he graduates, in the form of his student debt and no way to pay it. In the end, when masses of students have this, if it is all forgiven by the government, then the taxpayer pays for it, but, elsewhere in this book, I have explained why that leads to a downward spiral.

There are countless other examples, because there are countless other safety regulations where the government expects the free market to pay for safety standards that are imposed, where the safety standards make things more expensive so that the free market can't make a profit on it to pay for its existence, and the government does not itself pay for that benefit for the people. Whenever this happens, there is a good chance that, instead of a safer benefit existing, no benefit will exist at all.

What the liberals don't understand is that, if the money isn't there to pay for the benefit that they are supposedly providing to the poor, then they are just screwing the poor over, because if the benefit isn't paid for then it won't exist, instead nothing will exist and the poor will get nothing at all. These benefits do not exist by magic. If a poor woman can't become a prostitute, but needs an expensive medical procedure to survive, and she is denied the job where she could have made the money to pay for it, who will pay for it? The liberals are quick to spend other people's money, but not their own, and the liberal politicians behave that way too.

The socialists might say that everything I have said is true, but the government actually should pay for all these benefits: the government should give money to the poor woman instead of letting her become a prostitute, the government should pay for the poor person's legal fees, etc. The problem, then, becomes twofold: first, the government doesn't have the money to pay for this, and, if it raised taxes, not even all the rich taxpayers actually have the money to pay for every benefit in the liberal utopian dream world, but even attempting this would consume all the resources in the economy and destroy the economy.

Second, in the United States, as a practical matter, the free market has lobbyists and is never going to be forced to pay for these things, and the political will to pay for all these things at the taxpayer's expense is just not there in the United States, and hopefully never will be, and never should be.

Note that the problem would not be solved by merely printing more money to pay for these things: as I have explained, money represents value. No matter how much money that gets printed, for example, the doctors who perform the medical procedure for the poor woman, those doctors need food to eat and homes to live in, to say nothing of cash to pay off their med school student loans, this is what they get in return for the surgical procedure, that is traded to them as represented by the money that is paid by the woman for the operation, and she makes that money by working as a prostitute (for example, she has sex with a baker who then bakes the pizza that one of the doctors eats).

If the benefit of the poor woman not having to be a prostitute is to be paid for then whoever pays for it must make the value consumed by the doctors on behalf of the poor woman's medical operation. So, to pay for the benefit of laws banning prostitution in the name of protecting poor women from exploitation, actual new value would need to be created and given to the poor, not merely empty dollar bills.

The money that pays for something pays for the resources that are consumed to provide it, just as, when X buys B from A, C's D is consumed by A and is paid for by the Y that X made that is consumed by C, so that, for B to be paid for, X must make Y, or else someone else must make Y but then give Y to X for free as a gift without consuming anything in return for that.

In contrast, a libertarian solution might look like these:

1. Let Google and Facebook pay for the poor to have free access to Google and Facebook,

2. Let there be every possible job for the poor that the economy can support, even if some of these jobs are for unskilled uneducated workers and are low paying, because any job is better than no job, and if the worker starves to death then his employer loses him so there probably won't be that low of a wage,

3. Let the poor who can't afford the best lawyer hire a cheaper lawyer, if he chooses to do so, because he should be the one to decide if the risk of a bad cheap lawyer or having no lawyer at all is better for him, and

4. Let the poor who want high-paying jobs be free to become prostitutes and drug dealers, because the choice to conduct morally questionable behavior to make more money should be a personal ethical decision for each individual, not a decision imposed by the government, and there will always be some poor people who want the right to make money and to get rich at the expense of doing what other people consider sinful.

5. Let the free market handle student loans. Where there is a profit to be made for the lender on enabling a smart hard-working poor or middle class young person to go to school to get much better job skills, the free market will find and fund that education. If not, then the education doesn't pay for its own costs and is worthless. Let the poor person spend four years apprenticing at an entry level job and making money and learning practical job skills, and if they want to pay for night school or part-time college, let them be free to pay for it. The alternatives are cruel or even more cruel: it would be cruel to waste a ton of money by the government paying for these educations, but it is far more cruel to make the poor person have the ability to spend the student loan money, but then tie the debt around their neck and expect them to be held liable to pay a massive student loan debt that they are too poor to afford to pay, and for which the education was not great enough and they will never get such a good job because of it that their salary will pay off that debt.

The liberals will scream that I am denying the poor a basic human right, a college education. If they think that, then let them pay for it. With the $100,000 cost of a secondary education, let these liberals give all their money to charity, that still would not be enough for it, but at least they would no longer be hypocrites. The free market won't pay for it, and the government isn't paying for it, instead the poor are going to end up paying for it and, when they lack the funds to do so, declare bankruptcy, which is what happens when a person lacks the money to pay a debt. These liberals have good intentions that are paving the road to Hell for poor young people.

In every libertarian solution, the free market provides a cheaper alternative so that the poor can have at least something, which is better than nothing, and the poor are not forced to adopt that benefit that the free market makes available, and are free to instead choose nothing (to not become a prostitute and instead have no job) and to then face the consequences of that freely made choice to prefer nothing over what the market can afford to offer.

So, there are two possibilities that don't screw over the poor: one, pay for these benefits, meaning elect a socialist government in the United States, which will never happen and, if it did, would bankrupt the economy, or, two, don't mandate these benefits, and instead let the free market be free, and let freedom evolve into whatever benefits for the poor that can exist and can be paid for by the profit of the process of making and selling them. Anything else, and all such liberal paternalism, isn't merely absurd, it also totally screws over the poor and ruins the lives of the poor by denying them the benefits that actually can be paid for and that the market can afford.

Chapter Seventeen: Private Inefficiencies, Private Corrections

Let us assume that the free market is capable of errors. I will examine some errors which actually do exist. Then I will show how the free market is capable of correcting its own errors, in each example.

1. The mergers and acquisitions accounting error. Let us assume that there is a company named X, who makes Y, and X is worth $1 million. There is another company, A, that makes B, and A is worth $1 million. Let us assume that, in a merger or acquisition, X buys A. The way financial accounting is today, X will be able to report growth of $1 million, and its stock price on Wall Street will then go up to reflect that the investors now view X as being worth $2 million, not $1 million.

This is, I think, an error, for this reason: Y and B are still being produced, and, unless more Y or more B is produced, nothing has changed, so, if X is now worth $2 million, then A should be worth $0, and the collection known as X plus A should be worth $2 million but X plus A was already worth $2 million so no actual growth has happened. Yet Wall Street would view this as growth, and X's stock price would go up, over and above the $1 million that X presumably paid to buy all of A's stock.

The only exception is if efficiencies of scale make it cheaper for B and Y to be produced together, at one factory instead of two, or if X has better management than A and can produce more efficiently, then growth equal to the marginal increased efficiency would happen, but it probably could never be anywhere near $1 million of growth. Growth has happened from the point of view of X, but not from the point of view of Y and B, yet Y and B are where the profit comes from.

But let us consider how the free market could correct this error. X buys A, and then its stock price goes up. There are, for the sake of argument, no efficiencies of scale nor improved management. B and Y hold constant. But, then, it follows logically that X's profit from Y plus B will hold constant. At the point when the market realizes this, that there is no more growth, X's stock price will go down. If the market comes to believe that X's growth was phony, X's stock price could go way down. But what if the investors choose to never mark X's stock price down to reality? This ties into the next error and its free market correction.

2. The private inflation error. In recent years there has been a boom in private equity funding of software startups in Silicon Valley. Companies that have never made a profit and never will make a profit raise millions of dollars and are then acquired for hundreds of millions of dollars. Software entrepreneur founders walk away self-made millionaires having never produced any value that is objectively worth a million dollars. The "VCs", the venture capitalists, set the valuation of the company when they fund them. If a VC invests $10 million for a 33% stake, the startup is "worth" $30 million, even if it makes no profit. The VC himself chooses his funding and the percent of equity he will buy, and he thereby chooses his own valuation. In essence, he can arbitrarily decide how much money the startup is worth.

I have said that money represents value, and that when value goes up and money supply remains constant, that is private deflation. This is the reverse: if value is constant but the money amount goes up, that is private inflation. VCs cannot print physical paper dollar bills, but they can create money on an accounting record, and, in reality, the Federal Reserve also adds to the money supply by increasing the numbers of dollars listed in ledgers and records of the banks. When a VC raises the valuation of a startup, he is doing the exact same thing, increasing the amount of dollars per the value of the startup.

One VC can arbitrary set a company's valuation at $30 million for its first round of fundraising and take a 33% stake for $10 million, the next VC at the next round of fundraising can then set this same company's valuation at $100 million by buying a 33% stake for $33 million, or some big corporation can simply acquire the company for $100 million, and, if this happens, then on the books the first VC just made $23 million (the current value of his 33% minus what he paid for it) on the books, and yet nothing has actually been produced, X did not make Y, no money has been made by the company, and say, for example, that they make an app that will never make a profit.

Were this allowed to go unchecked, it would be a bubble, and, when a bubble bursts, there is panic, a run on the banks, a recession, etc. But can the private sector, the free market, correct its own error? I think it can, and, over the long term, it does and necessarily will. The mistake is to look at it from the point of view of the startup and the Y made by startup X, when it should be looked at from the point of view of the investor's money and the startup X creating investment opportunity Y which is purchased by the investor for the cost of the equity.

When the investor invests $10 million, he is buying the opportunity to profit if the company succeeds. According to the choice theory of value, what is bought is objectively worth what a buyer chooses to pay for it in a free market. Apple, Facebook and Google are all worth over $100 billion; if the investor thinks that the startup's app has a 1% chance of success and, if successful, has a 1% chance of being the next Google, that opportunity in itself is objectively worth $10 million (1 percent times 1 percent times $100 billion). Thus, even an app that doesn't have a prayer in Hell of ever making one cent of profit might actually be worth a lot of money, not as a vehicle for private inflation, but as a legitimate investment. Who is to say, then, what that investment should really be worth? According to XYAB, it is for the investor to decide, but, if he turns out to be wrong in the context of the marketplace, he will bear the loss that results from his mistake.

Let's say that the investor invests $10 million at a $30 million valuation in a software startup that makes an app that makes bird calls for duck hunters. Let us assume that the market for this app is small and the app will never get many users and the users will not pay very much for it and so it will actually never make money. Let's say that it obviously will never make money, but there is a tiny, tiny chance that it could squeeze out some sort of profit in a few years, and that there is some economic data according to which something that is similar to it, an app that creates dog whistles for dog owners, has actually been commercially successful.

When the investor gives the startup $10 million, that is money, but it represents a value that is given to the business as resources to consume in the process of developing and selling the app. These resources are made by someone: by the investor, or by people who are paid by the investor in a XYAB trade that ends in wealth created by the investor, who, presumably, made the money he invests, or inherited money to invest from someone else, his father or grandfather (or mother or grandmother) who made that money. Hence, ultimately, the money is backed by value created by the investor.

If the app makes no money and the startup dies, the investor loses $10 million. That represents real value, that he created and owned, that gets destroyed if his investment goes bust. There was, from the investor's point of view, a chance the duck hunter app would be worth $1 billion in five years, and this was worth a risk of $10 million of loss. This is the choice theory of value: what the risk's worth is chosen by what the investor chooses to buy it for, not what the actual duck hunt app is "objectively" worth.

But what if a bubble forms and then bursts and it destroys the economy? If a bubble bursts, the analysis of what happens should be done, not for society as a whole, but for each company and investor individually, and, in the end, each person who suffers loss will lose what they chose to put at risk, be that risk stupid or clever.

In a libertarian economy, if a bubble forms and the bubble bursts, the rich investors are the ones who lose everything, and society is not the one who pays for it (more on that below, and why that has not happened historically in our liberal/conservative economy).

We can assume, for another example, that the investor helps the startup get acquired for $100 million, and the socialists will say that the investor spent $10 million but got $100 million and made $90 million of profit by promoting a fraudulent piece of garbage and society will bear the costs when that garbage is marked to market at its real value of, for example, the $20,000 that a piece of garbage app is really worth instead of the $100 million VC valuation.

But, again, there is a company, that is rich, that made $100 million and which chose to spend $100 million to buy that risk-reward profile opportunity. That company will take a $100 million loss if the duck hunt app fails. If it can't afford a $100 million loss, it will go bankrupt, and its owners, not society, will bear that loss. Giant companies have gone bankrupt in the last hundred years, plenty of them, and the personal responsibility is real, it is not mere capitalist propaganda. The rich cannot keep passing the buck of loss when the trash is marked to market down the line and ultimately pass it off to society, because it ends up in the hands of whoever bought it, and they lack the ability to distribute it to the taxpayer.

Of course, if massive companies all lose $100 million on one awful day it can lead to massive bankruptcies and layoffs and start a recession. But, when the bankruptcies clear and the debris and rot of stupid investors is cleared away, the smart people who remained in business pick up the pieces and move on--as happened with the Great Recession, except that would have gone better if Obama the liberal had not made the incorrect argument that it is the government's job to bail out bad investors and given a gigantic payment to Wall Street to "bail out" the idiots who lost billions of dollars on subprime home mortgages.

Massive bankruptcies punish the stupid investors and owners, not "society," and the government did not need to bail out Wall Street or Detroit to "save" the economy during the Great Recession, as the free market would have recalibrated supply and demand and ownership of capital from stupid to smart and been better off. But the big government liberals are always looked for an opportunity for government to interfere in the economy, even when it inures to the benefit of Wall Street. We libertarians unanimously opposed the bailout, although both the big business Wall Street conservatives and the big government liberals supported it, and we are consistent and have integrity in the policy I have presented.

The liberal argument that society pays for the irresponsibility of the rich is only true if the government bails the rich out instead of letting them go bankrupt, so perhaps Obama sought to fulfil his own leftist prophecy with the taxpayer-funded bailout. The Obama bailout, not free market capitalism, explains why society paid for the burst bubble of the Great Recession, and there has been ample libertarian economic research, by Milton Friedman and Murray Rothbard among others, showing that the Federal Reserve, the state-owned bank, was to blame for society bearing the losses of the bubble bursting in the Great Depression. In a normal libertarian economy, private inflation is not a threat to be regulated, because the perpetrators are the ones who suffer the losses, not society, if and when the bubble bursts.

One may think I am violating my own choice theory of value by saying that, if the investor buys the investment opportunity for $10 million, it might "objectively" be worthless. But remember in that chapter I said that if X buys B for $50, but across the river and through the woods there are a thousand people who are buying Bs for $1, then the market prices B at $1, and X overpaid because B is not really worth $50. It is worth $1, although X thinks it is worth $50 and, in the absence of the woods market, it could have been worth $50 on that basis alone.

In Wall Street, in theory at least, the price you pay to buy a stock is what you are paying for a dividend stream that this public company will pay to you over the life of your stock ownership. Dividends are paid out of profits, which is why stock price goes up when profits go up, because the investors buy the stocks that have higher profits, driving the share price up. In Wall Street, there are, according to some estimates, at least eleven thousand stocks in the market. These have an average valuation of what profits are worth in terms of share price, and trust me, it is not a valuation of $30 million for an unrealistic chance at a tiny profit. It is according to this valuation that a valuation of $30 million for a worthless duck hunting app is overpriced and not worth it.

When I say that the valuation will be marked to market and will be forced down, I mean that, eventually and inevitably, the company must raise capital in the stock market, at which point it will compete against the valuation of the other eleven thousand companies, forcing it down from fantasy into reality. When that happens, and it is inevitable because no man may defy the market and survive, that difference between the old valuation and the new valuation is a loss of money, at least on the books, which someone pays for by taking that loss on their balance sheet and bank account.

But, in a free market, the investor who took the risk and chose to buy the investment takes the loss, because the owned equity is on his books. No one other than him bears the loss. He would also be the one who profits if the company succeeds, which is perfectly fair, because this potential for loss and possibility of gain is the risk-reward profile that he decided to buy, putting his money at risk in order to get a possible reward.

3. Monopolies. When a big company acquires its main competitor, it can charge a monopoly price and price-gouge the consumer. When supply goes down but demand remains constant, price must go up, at which point some people at the previous level can no longer afford the product. I do not deny this. Indeed, I embrace that analysis. But, if this happens, and there is a market for a product at a cheaper price, then some new competitor will always enter the market and undercut the monopoly. This will always happen because in capitalism, entrepreneurs seek profits, and this is a natural profit-making opportunity.

The leftists say that, in practice, this can't happen, you can't enter a market without capital, and there are barriers to entry. The theory of "barriers to entry," is a myth, no such thing exists. And if the opportunity for profit is there, then capital can't afford not to fund it. The rich get rich from profits, not from big size. Some rich businessmen practice, and believe, what I refer to as "reverse Marxism": they believe that ownership of the means of production exploits the poor, and have decided to try to get rich by intentionally exploiting the poor and owning the means of production. But these people are wrong, and Marxist theory is not true, whether it be for the benefit of the Marxists or of the reverse Marxists. Such corrupt businessmen who do not compete on value or price and instead seek to dominate on size do not "make" money, they do not create wealth. Therefore in a XYAB free market, they will lose to their smaller but hungrier and smarter competitors, inevitably and necessarily over the long term, because once chance factors out over the long term money is a reflection of value produced.

As such, there is no real need for antitrust law. That having been said, there are statist government regulations that the rich use to stifle competition. In an economy that is *not* a free market, there can be barriers to entry, created by regulations or the cost of legal compliance, at which point a little bit of antitrust enforcement might not be such a bad thing for the consumer, but pure libertarian XYAB economics would be a better long term solution.

Chapter Eighteen: The Freedom to Buy Things vs. the Freedom to Buy Government Favoritism

There is a libertarian position which holds that a person with more money should be free to buy more things than a person with less money, and that this is not unfair. Provided that the money is made, and earned, I agree. But there is a thorny issue that develops as a result of this position. Let us consider some scenarios to see it:

Case 1. A rich person buys something that a poor person can't afford. Say, for example, that a rich person with a good job can afford to buy a diamond ring for their spouse, but a poor person can't afford to. A libertarian would say that this is fair.

Case 2. The government creates a benefit, and, by laws passed by the government, the benefit is given to the rich but not to the poor. Say, for example, that a rich person owns a business, a store, and there is another store across the street that competes against him. This rich person gives big political donations to the campaign of the local mayor, and the mayor then passes a city ordinance that changes the zoning laws so that the store across the street must move and can no longer do business there, effectively eliminating competition against the rich donor's business. Real libertarians would say that this is grossly unfair, and mere crony capitalism, a violation of free market principles.

Now, every libertarian will support case 1, but any true libertarian would say that he or she opposes case 2, and that case 2 is pure statism, which every real libertarian is against. Many libertarians would even refer to case 2 as fascism. The government action in case 2 to create and bestow a benefit is inherently done by force and in violation of freedom, which violates the core libertarian non-aggression axiom, that every libertarian follows in one flavor or another.

But what about case 3?

Case 3. The government creates a benefit and sells it at a price that only the rich can afford to pay.

Here we have the rich being able to freely spend their money and buy something, which is like case 1. The poor cannot afford it, like case 1. But here we also have government force and coercion that creates a benefit that the free market did not (and most likely cannot) create, like case 2. So, is case 3 more like case 1, or more like case 2?

In practice, I believe that libertarians are very confused on this issue, and some would be in favor of the legality of case 3 and do not consider it unfair, while others would call case 3 a type of statism and unfair and oppose it.

To think this through, let's consider two examples:

A. In primary education, the rich can afford to send their kids to private schools, the poor can't afford to. That is like case 1. But the public schools, which are horrible and failing and trap kids in poverty by giving them bad educations, are state-owned, created by the government, and the mandatory schooling of the kids in these horrible schools is mandated by law. That is like case 2. So, education is a case of case 3.

Is the educational system in the United States fair, from a libertarian point of view? Is it fair for rich kids to get good educations when the poor do not? Some libertarians say this is fair, it is just the rich spending money that the poor lack, like 1, and it isn't the fault of the rich that the rich kids benefit from a state-owned system that kills the poor kids' educations. Other libertarians say that the public educational system is contaminated by statism and that the government control of education renders the entire system unfair, and unfair to the poor kids who suffer under it.

B. In the law, the rich can afford to hire good lawyers. The poor can't. That is fair, according to libertarians, it is case 1, just freedom to spend money. But, scientific research has indicated that, in the

United States, there is systemic racism, in that studies and research show that white people and rich people get more favorable outcomes from judges than poor people or black people in cases that were identical in every measurable detail other than race and class. To some libertarians, racism and oppression against individuals by government-appointed lords, i.e. the judges, is a clear example of case 2, it is statism.

But then, to make this clear as case 3, the rich and whites who have better lawyers tend to get much better outcomes. Are these better outcomes because of having more money to hire better lawyers, which is fair, or because of racism and classism by judges who are supposed to be neutral, which is unfair?

I personally believe that case 3 is like case 2, and is statism, and is unfair, and that libertarians should oppose this, and this is not just the freedom of the rich to be rich, it is in fact the "freedom" of the rich to pay the government in return for force used on their behalf, which we libertarians refer to as "crony capitalism." I think that, in a shades of gray scenario, where there is a mix of case 1 and case 2 (and I do not deny that some case 1 is present in case 3) that, unless it is a pure, perfect, clean, spotless case of case 1, if there is *any* contamination of case 2 in case 3, if the government interferes in any way, then we libertarians must say that the government corrupted the entire affair, and made case 3 like case 2, and we must oppose case 3 and call for reform until the state's contamination is cleansed away and we could say with confidence that the thing is entirely case 1.

So, no, I do not think that the American primary educational system is fair to the poor kids, not because the rich kids can afford better schools, but because the government has created a state-imposed system where rich kids succeed and poor kids fail. Letting the rich buy a government-created benefit whose very existence defies the free market is more like bestowing a statist benefit upon the rich than letting a rich person buy something that was freely made in the unregulated private sector, as I see it.

If the arena of education were fully deregulated, and we had school choice, then I would see nothing wrong with rich kids going to private schools that poor kids can't afford. But, if education was deregulated, it would also be true that there would be educational entrepreneurs who would enter the education market and make a profit from finding ways to sell high quality educations to the poor, perhaps by using accurate educational tests to identify smart poor kids and then selling them great educations on credit at high interest loans to be paid off during the course of their career as successful adults. And, with school choice, the poor kids would be free to choose good schools instead of being forced to attend bad schools at the point of the government's gun.

Some recent innovation at the college educational level with private schools that teach software engineering on private student loans shows that a deregulated educational system would perform better (although college is not yet fully deregulated either), but, sadly, by the time the kids from bad k-12 schools reach college age their hopes and dreams and IQs are already destroyed.

The utopia of school choice is a far cry from today's system, where the teacher's unions control the schools and use a seniority-based system designed to deprive teachers of any sort of reward based on competence or success, all the while mandating standardized tests that don't measure anything relevant to IQ or skills and then imposing educations throughout k-12 school that are designed to teach to these tests, not to reality. Even the middle class kids in public schools are actually suffering from this system, while the kids in the truly poor schools suffer from this, plus school buildings that are neglected and full of rot and mold and dangerous, and a stigma from the name of their high school that will scare away any good college admissions officer and any high-wage employer. And, with all this, the poor kid is assigned their school by the state and forced to attend it.

Thus, while it is true that the rich are not to blame for the educational system, it is also true that the rich kids who attend private schools enjoy a huge advantage over the poor kids, in practical reality, precisely because of the statist government interference in the system, as compared to the reality that would exist in a perfectly free market. That, in my mind, is not fair to the poor kids. It is an unfairness that is caused by statism, not by being rich, but it is an unfairness that inherently benefits only the rich.

We can, and must, oppose this. Opposing it does no harm to our credentials as libertarians and champions of economic freedom, any more than it would harm a libertarian's credibility to oppose fascism or crony capitalism, both of which also benefit the rich. Furthermore, the only solution that I call for is school choice and a deregulation of k-12 education, which is already a basic libertarian stance.

So, too, in the law: if the judges are racists and classists, that must be rooted out and cleansed and reformed, and if the law firms that represent the rich and powerful take advantage of this then they, too, are corrupt and crooked. For example, rich and powerful lawyers are often friends with all the judges in their areas of practice, and are essentially selling their nepotism and influence to the rich clients of these lawyers. Yes, the poor can't afford to hire these lawyers, and the rich can, so this is a benefit of being able to spend money. But there is more to it than merely having money and being able to buy something.

Statist corruption is baked into this system. This practice is corrupt, because a neutral and impartial judge is a legal right of all people. It is bribery, and it should be rooted out, and eliminating this will not hinder capitalist freedom nor onset statism in any way whatsoever. Having a fair legal system will not prevent rich people from buying good lawyers. Remember, we libertarians want to allow *economic* inequality to exist, but we believe in *political* equality, which includes equality before the law.

The solution for this problem would not be easy, but good first steps would be: having the judge be blind to the race and class and identity of the litigants, such as by putting the litigants in a closed room and communicating with the judge via speech to text on a screen that the judge reads without ever seeing their names or faces; banning or limiting social contacts between lawyers and judges, both in and outside of the courthouses; having independent investigations that examine judges for biases and impose recusal in cases where the judge would be probably be biased as an honest person would evaluate it.

If justice is blind then the judge does not need to know who the litigants are nor even who the lawyers are, and technology has evolved that could be used so that a judge could rule on a case in a neutral and impartial manner by examining evidence and reading a transcript of the lawyer's argument on a computer screen, without seeing the defendant's faces or hearing the lawyer's voices. In such a system, more money would still buy better lawyers who make better arguments to the judge, but the rich as such would not receive bias from the justice system. There would be constitutional hurdles to overcome with this, but it could be done as an opt in option, and I think it can be done.

That having been said, the liberals take advantage of our confusion. They say that case 3 *and case 1* are both like case 2. This is simply not true. For capitalism to exist, for supply and demand to be efficient, greater values must cost a greater price, just as cheaper values cost fewer dollars. This way, resources that chase profits are correctly assigned to make more desirable goods and services, in proportion to the price signals that buyers send to the market. That, from the point of view of economics, is as it should be.

Chapter Nineteen: The Sale

In XYAB, in the first diagram, X trades Y to A in return for B, or, in the triangle of trade, in return for $5. Throughout this book I have focused on the production of Y and the consumption of B. But there is a step in between the trade of Y for B or the purchase of Y for a sale price of $5, and this a significant step worth examining. This step can be called "making the sale."

One of the biggest objections to XYAB as a justification for libertarianism is that the sale contaminates the process whereby everyone gets what they want and ends up happy. A good salesman, the socialists say, could sell garbage to a poor victim for a high price. The choice theory of value is flawed because Y is not priced in terms of B, but in terms of X's ability to make the sale.

This is not true, but it has a grain of truth to it. In terms of the law, I support provisions against fraud, so that A knows what he is buying and the sale can be voided if X lied to A, although mere puffery and bragging is not necessarily an outright lie. Laws mandating honesty in labels, honesty in sales information, disclosures of price and other factors, etc., can all be appropriate as extensions of the principle that fraud violates XYAB, that a lie told to a buyer during the sale is not a legitimate part of the XYAB triangle of trade.

That having been said, even without fraud as a possibility, in the XYAB system, there is a problem, which is that, until X pays $5 for B and consumes B, X isn't going to know if he likes B or not. This, as I see it, is the trust issue. X can infer B's quality from A's good work, or from A's sales pitch, or from stories told by other people who have bought and/or used B, but X cannot know until he consumes B, by which point in time B is consumed and can no longer be returned for a refund. Perfect, rationally justified trust cannot exist prior to consumption. The sale must persuade the buyer to, in a sense, make a leap of faith. How can this be done, or justified as logical?

Capitalism has already evolved ways to solve this problem. For example, professional reviewers or consumer reviews rate a product, and X can draw an analogy between himself and the reviewer's opinion of the product. There are also "try before you buy" and "money back guarantee" sales, or, even without those, returns policies. Moreover, there is a model according to which a new business operates at a loss and sells the product at a low price to gain consumer trust, and then, once trust is established, the business raises the price and makes their profit.

In the end, the only way X can know for sure is to consume B. But this is a risk that X must bear. This trust issue is basic to economics, in fact it is basic to how human knowledge and human learning works, and is not something that can be legislated away, because humans learn about something only by physically experiencing it. We are not all-knowing nor do we possess mystical insight. It is simply impossible for X to have perfect trust in B until after he buys and consumes it. But perfect knowledge is far too demanding a standard for economics, or the socialists, to expect in human behavior. The inferences, and risks, and experiments of trial and error, that will really happen in a free market are a sufficient solution to the trust problem.

For X to buy B, there must be the creation of B by A, but A must also make the sale. I believe that making the sale is conceptually and theoretically distinct from B, and from A creating B as such. The skills of production are not necessarily the skills of making the sale. In a division of labor economy, there are firms, where someone makes B, and another person's job is to sell B to X, so that a hard worker or design genius can make B, while a fast-talking charismatic salesman can make the sale of B to X for $5. The sale can even itself be thought of as another D made by a salesman C, and be studied in terms of the supply of and demand for salesmen and the sales they make.

One may even think of the firm itself as a salesman, of a sort, in that management collects the work of diverse individuals in order to create something that no one individual could have made by himself, and then makes a sale of that super-product at a large scale to a buyer that could only be made by the firm as an organizer of separate individuals into a whole, where the product required many people to produce, and making the sale required that product, and required a team of salesmen that the management organized. Making the sale between X and A can be thought of as two individuals, or as two firms, or as a firm to an individual, or as employees selling to their labor to a firm which then resells that labor unified into one product to a buyer.

From one point of view, the production of value, the creation of wealth, is what drives capitalism, but from a practical point of view, making the sale is what guides and motivates business, as every A really only cares about chasing X's $5. The good that is done by XYAB, e.g. for the upward spiral, is unintentional, as Adam Smith observed in his Invisible Hand theory.

None of this analysis of the role of the sale in trades negates my choice theory of value that B is objectively worth $5. Making the sale is merely a step, a natural part, of the XYAB process.

Chapter Twenty: The Finite Economy

The pool of value in the economy is finite. Therefore, any given person might take out a little bit more than he puts in, or put in a little bit more than he takes out, but the whole thing, as a whole, must balance, because value is just a set of physically existing objects in physical reality, in a finite sum. We can expect everything to be consumed, but you can't consume something that doesn't exist, so the sums will all match up, production will equal consumption.

This is relevant because, the question then becomes, if the government spends money that it did not make, then what value is being consumed? The answer must be that, in a capitalist economy, value is produced, and some of it is consumed by end consumers, and some of it is consumed by the process of production, to invest in future production. Think the seed stock of a farmer, for example. Once all of the value to consume as end consumer consumption is used up, the investment capital is what must be consumed, because there isn't any other value in the economy to consume, and the government's dollars are buying things that are really getting consumed by people.

This leaves us with a scary, terrifying thought. Seed stock is necessary for next year's harvest. The investments in production, in research and technology, building factories, starting new businesses, etc., is necessary, not merely for economic growth, but for economic survival. In a true crisis, where the government spends too much, people's lives have become dependent on that spending, and the government runs out of enough money to spend–and they say this could happen in the USA by the end of the Twenty-First Century with the Social Security/Medicare/Medicaid entitlement bomb–society may find itself trapped in a position where it consumes its investment and destroys and bankrupts the economy's long-term survival, like a farmer who runs out of seed to plant, or there will not be enough value created for people to consume and there will be mass deaths of the people on welfare who no longer have value to consume, e.g. food to eat.

This is what I would refer to as a downward spiral, the opposite of my upward spiral. All made possible by the good intentions of the statist government politicians!

The principle of the finite economy also explains why socialist economics fails as a matter of necessity. If you consume what has not been produced, then inevitably, even if you do begin with vast resources to consume–even if you tax all the wealth of the rich, and if that is a vast, huge amount of wealth–consuming this wealth without replacing it will inevitably use it all up, it will then all be consumed and no production will replace it, and, when all the wealth is consumed, the economy goes bankrupt. This is what is meant by "there isn't enough money in the world to pay for the leftist utopia": obviously a government can print more money, but it can't create more value to consume by magic or fiat.

Only a government organized according to the principle of XYAB economics can match production to consumption, because, in a XYAB economy, for every Y that A consumes A must produce a B for X to consume to match it, because that is how it works. In XYAB, X, in order to consume B, must produce Y, precisely that Y which A wants to consume, for which A chooses to trade away B to X.

Chapter Twenty One: Work, Luck, Context and Ownership

Do the rich exploit the working class? They force them to work long hours for low pay, and the workers starve to death if they refuse.

That, at least, is the leftist narrative. Upon analysis, it disintegrates. For an employer whose revenues are fixed relative to its wage costs, long hours and low pay maximizes profits. Those profits enable the employer to stay in business, so that the job continues to exist, and the money is there to pay the salary, i.e., in XYAB, the money is *made* to pay the worker's salary.

If the worker does not like this, he is free to quit his job and seek employment elsewhere. If a better job exists, he can seek it. If a better job exists but he is not qualified for it, he can seek further education or better job skills. If a better job does not exist, then he can't do any better, and, in order for a better job to exist when no such job currently exists, the money to pay for it would have to be made, meaning that either there is a profit-making opportunity somewhere that could create a better job, in which case the market probably will create it, or already has created it somewhere else, or else, if the market cannot justify a better job for this worker, if there is nothing this worker can make that some employer could profit off of to pay a wage for shorter hours and higher salary, then, for the worker to get a better job, someone else would have to pay for it at a loss–either by a person paying the worker more than the money he was making by doing his job, which would be charity, or by the government paying the worker to do a job for which the work done does not make the money and justify the salary, i.e. does not make the money of the salary. In that case the taxpayer pays for it, value is essentially taken from the taxpayer and given to the worker, and the idea that this is a "job" or a "salary" ceases to be taken seriously, it becomes mere welfare, and a joke farce of someone going through the motions of doing a job without generating a profit to pay for it.

The leftists will say that I am making a laughable joke when I say that, in practice, a worker could quit his job to seek a better one, or get better job skills–they are too poor to afford to and would starve to death if they take that risk, they are stuck, trapped. It may be true that a given individual may have little chance of doing better, may have to take an extreme risk to climb the ladder, may put himself and his family in danger of starvation to do so, and may hate and suffer from the working conditions of the job he finds himself stuck in. At times in my own life, I have been in exactly this situation, and hated and loathed it as much as any leftist could claim. I am not a rich spoiled brat and am well aware of the way things work in the real world.

My answer to this is simple: The worker exists in the context of an economy with a certain set of people, resources, and opportunities. He is free to make his choices and receive the good or bad results of those decisions, but only within the context of that economy, which means: in this reality that you and I live in. Every human being is born into a context of luck and chance and reality and physical limitations. To change any of this is to fill a lack of money with money, but the worker himself is not making the money to do this, so someone else would have to be forced to make a value and give it to the worker to consume, for the context to be improved for the worker.

If the worker wants a reality that does not exist, he wants to dream up a new reality and impose it onto this one, and he wants other people to pay for it, too. In theory, this is a defiance of reality, in practice, it becomes impossibly expensive, because there is no one to pay for it, and, if someone else could, there is no reason why they should have money stolen from them, that they *made*, to pay for this worker who doesn't pay for his own salary.

XYAB is relevant here because it shows that, when a person has a job, their salary, those dollar bills, are made by the work that they do, that makes a profit for their employer. The worker makes Y, an hour of doing work, and sells it to the employer for $10, the employer then sells it to other people, and the worker's $10 then buys something, say a sandwich, from those other people. A job is not magic, it is making money, and the money of the salary is made by the work that is done, in a trade of the employee's labor for the employer's salary, where what the employer gets out of it is a profit on whatever the end product is that is sold. Absent making money, absent earning one's salary by X making Y, there isn't really a job. A decent, honorable man with self-respect wants a job where he earns his salary, not a fake, phony "job" where the government, really the taxpayer, pays for him to go through the motions and pretend that he is being productive. To a worker with honesty and honor, he exists within the context, and limits himself to that, because that is the only world wherein he can pay for himself.

The concept of "context" is significant here, because I meant what I said: if the worker does not like his job, he is free to seek a better one. The leftist then says that no better one is easily obtainable. From this, the leftist draws the conclusion that tax and spend should "create" one. I draw a different conclusion, namely, that the worker has run up against the boundaries of his context, and this must be accepted by him, because a person can only reasonably be expected to act within their context, and cannot act outside of it. You do not get to choose your context, you only get to choose what you do within it.

To articulate the concept of context further, let us consider the Rawlsian notion that people should view economics and politics from the point of view of someone who has not yet been born. A person could be born into good luck, and wealth, or into bad luck, and poverty. This is true, and the luck and chance that one is born into is what I would refer to as that person's context. But I think that the actual progression into a person's being is more like a series of steps: one begins from the point of view of a soul, then is born into a context, then from that context emerges you, the person that you are, you then have free will and a set of talents, you make decisions, from your talents and your decisions but within the boundaries of your context you do work, that work makes money, and you then spend that money and consume the result of the trades of what you produced i.e. the work that you did.

Rawls, and the leftists, look at things from the point of view of focusing on the first step, being born into a context. I prefer to focus on a later step, you doing work to make money, by which point the context is a given and can't be changed. You make money using what the context gives you, using what is available in the context. After the point at which you are you, you can't change the context, the context is a given from within which you must make your decisions. Thus, a person should not be thinking about changing their context, which really means, altering reality, they should be thinking about their choices and decisions.

Luck and chance are inherent in reality. If you are born into bad luck, then, yes, I'm sorry, you had bad luck. But that is what it is, it can't be changed.

The leftist will then say, but if everyone has bad luck, then that is a social problem, and the few who have good luck should be taxed to pay for correcting the bad luck of the masses. So let us then examine this theory, that good luck should be taxed to equalize bad luck–but let's do it from a XYAB point of view.

Let us assume that, on average, as things average out, when a productive rich person makes $1 million, half of that is due to work, and half of that is due to the good luck of having been born into a context that makes this possible (either having been born rich, or having been born poor but with the opportunity to get a better job). So let's tax $500,000 of that $1 million. The problem arises when we try to use XYAB to analyze what Y was created that is going to pay for that $500,000 worth of dollar bills that was taken as taxes. When we go to collect it, we see that, true to form, X created Y, and Y is there, it is a thing that X created. If this is a productive rich person, he created the Y, or if he inherited it then one of his ancestors created Y and gave it to him. Upon the examination of Y itself, we do not see "good luck," we see Y. And, upon looking at the creation of Y, we see X creating it, we do not see "good luck" creating it.

Indeed, if good luck had created it, we would have expected it to have been just sitting there in the context waiting to be taken and consumed, with no work necessary to create it at all. But this is not true, and this is not what XYAB teaches. Thus, this theory that we should tax good luck to equalize bad luck, true to Rawls and leftism, collapses into the Marxist school of economics, that the means of production create wealth automatically, the vast wealth is just sitting there waiting to be distributed, with only the rich's fence standing between you and it. This is Marxism but it substitutes the concept of "good luck" that the rich inherit for "the means of production" that the rich own, as if this magical thing, not people, are what creates value. This is not a correct theory of economics, as, I hope, you have learned from reading this book.

According to XYAB, good luck doesn't make money, people make money. The money that is made is really the value that is created. When one spends a dollar, one can only consume value that was created. So, by definition, if a government benefit is to be paid by the taxpayer, it is paid for by the production of the productive rich, not the good luck of the lazy high status rich. The lazy rich don't make any value that could be consumed, as the leftist would be forced to concede according to his own internal logic. If the lazy high status rich don't create any value, then there is no value on their account that can be consumed. If the government taxes wealth at a 50% tax rate to capture the 50% of wealth due to good luck or owned by the lazy evil rich, but 100% of the tax money is given to people and results in real value being consumed, then 100% of that money must come from money made by productive rich, because they are the only ones who actually create value, and all money spent is real existing value that gets consumed.

The high status rich who are lazy and get rich due to good luck, indeed any of the "get money" rich, be they lucky or rich heirs or actual crooks and thieves and con artists, own dollar bills but make no money. Yet, when a benefit is paid, value is consumed, and that value was produced by the taxpayer. So "tax the evil rich" will necessarily always result in taxing the good "make money" rich, even if it is intended to tax the evil "get money" high status rich or merely to tax the good luck away from the rich to the proportional extent that their making money was due to good luck.

If a worker spends $5 that the government gave him, he buys a sandwich and eats it, someone made that money, someone made that sandwich, it was the tax payer, and this means that some rich person had to make something, for example a retail space to rent for the sandwich shop, which the sandwich shop owner then spends that $5 (plus money from all his other sales) to get, thus completing the triangle of trade. If money is spent, then resources are consumed, which requires that resources were produced, by the person who "made" the money that was spent. So taxing the rich proportionate to the extent that wealth is due to good luck, on the theory that fairness can equalize good luck and bad luck, collapses into a contradiction.

The socialists would say that they seek to tax, not what was created, but the inherited wealth of the rich heirs, which has been just sitting there for decades or centuries. But this, too, was created: someone's parents or grandparents created it and then gave it to them, so it was created and is legitimately owned, not from the point of view of the heir, but from the point of view of the creator's right to give what they created as gift to whomever they choose.

The socialist then asserts that the vast wealth of the rich was not created, it was just an accretion or accumulation of society, which the rich appropriated. This is obviously not true. In the United States, six hundred years ago, this land was nothing more than empty land, some forests, some mountains, some buffalo, and a few scattered Native American tribes. Everything that is in the United States today, above that baseline level, every factory, every mansion, every diamond necklace, was created by someone, and either they own it, or they gave it to their heirs, who gave it to their heirs, so that there is an unbroken line of a legitimate creator who made a legitimate gift to an heir, who thereby inherits the property rightly under XYAB.

Furthermore, XYAB holds that wealth is dynamic, not static, and value must be continuously created, for it all atrophies over time, albeit at varying rates, and so must be constantly renewed by active productivity, or else must cease to exist. The rich cannot create wealth and have their heirs just sit on it forever; profits must be made newly each year or else a company will die, and each year work must be done to turn a profit against fierce competition. So, yes, the analysis that taxes targeting the lazy heirs will actually pull value exclusively from the productive rich, is true.

Here I will make the somewhat counterintuitive argument that capitalism is fair and equal for the people who get good luck or bad luck in their context. For the worker, just like for the rich person, XYAB is an accurate explanation of their economic existence: even the lowliest janitor makes money, his salary is equal to the work that he does as priced by supply and demand in the market, the janitor too makes his money, the worker makes money. So, in that sense, XYAB sees equality between rich and poor.

Also, in the context, to take Rawls to his logical conclusion, everyone is born into good or bad luck, but, from the Rawlsian point of view, everyone had an equal chance to be born lucky or into bad luck. For this idea, say that one goes into a casino to play Blackjack. The rules of the casino are the same for everyone who plays the game, even though a few people will get lucky and walk away with money, and many will have bad luck and lose money. But contrast this with a casino where the deck is stacked with fake cards. In the latter case, the game is unfair, but in the former case, the game is fair, even though it is a game of chance with good luck or bad luck. The rules of the game, and the odds, were the same, were equal, for every player.

I say this not to say that making money is like winning in a casino, but, rather, to say that being born into good luck is like winning in a casino, that the context is the casino. If one does not like the casino as such, then one should leave, although to leave the context is to leave reality, and can't be done, absent, in a sense, suicide.

In reality, the only thing you can take for granted is what you would have had if you had been born in a desert island–air, some land to stand on, and nothing else. Everything that you experience above that is a gift, created by someone else, that you benefit from.

You stand on the shoulders of giants, and should not take what you have for granted, and demand to be given more at other people's expense. A person is ethical, not because of what they are given, but because of what they do with what they're given. You stand on the shoulders of giants, but the giants don't do the work for you, you do the work. A worker is defined, not by his context, but by what he does with it. The context does not make your money for you, instead, you make money using what the context gives you. In a sense, the context is the resources that are put into you, and you are the process that transforms the context into wealth, into consumable value, to make money.

A person takes substance out of nature and mixes his labor with it; he creates and is responsible for the result of this, and thereby owns it. This is the basic Locke theory of property, which is still true today. Except that in the modern era, every resource on Earth is already owned, so the nature that you take substance out of is actually the context. You take the situation that you are born into and whatever it gives you to work with, and you make things out of it, either making the most that you can of what you were given, or not doing your best and being lazy and making less than that.

It is a complicated thing to say that being given a better context would make a person happy if he is sad to begin with, it is a difficult thing to say that money actually buys happiness, but, in order to be a *good* person, I can say that all that can be asked of one is that one make the best of one's context, that one do as much as one can with the situation one was born into; more cannot be asked of a person and would be of no ethical significance. It is also true that if, instead of fighting the fight to be a good person within one's context, one instead rejects and rebels against the context itself, one is, in a sense, giving up on the fight, and instead complaining about having had to fight a tough battle to begin with.

The context, if you are born into bad luck, can be cruel. But life itself, is, and can be, cruel–reality is a tough place in which to live, this is not a perfect world, this is not an *easy* world in which to live, and life is tough, and being a human being is not easy. It is not clear that any species could ever exist in a world that was easy to live in, because, if resources were not scarce, they would be consumed until they reached the point at which they were scarce–and then, everywhere, a poor person's life would suck and it would require a huge risk to try to get a better job.

Given that this is a tough reality and a tough planet on which to survive, there is no reason why finding a good job should be easy, or why we would expect it to be easy or to have the potential to be easy. But "life," and "the world", and "reality", in this sense, is another name for the context. Life is tough, but the leftists who say that the context should be changed, are saying that life should be easy, and that we can change reality so that life is nice and easy and everyone gets the equivalent of being born into lots and lots of good luck. That *might* be a reality somewhere, but it is not this reality, it is not the reality that you and I live in, and the leftists lack the power to change the fundamental nature of this reality, although they can certainly bankrupt the economy in their quest to try.

Do the poor live horrible lives? Yes. Are they entitled to be given a better context, if they don't make the money to create one for themselves? No. Then why are the rich entitled to happy lives? But being *entitled* is precisely what the rich are not–the rich are happy because they got good luck (to be born rich) which is a matter of chance, which is random, not entitlement, which is necessary and guaranteed.

In a libertarian utopia of contract vs. status the rich are not entitled to be rich and can fall down at any time. Rich and poor play by the same rules of the casino: be born on planet Earth and either someone gives you money, you make money yourself, or you're poor, because money, to exist, must be made by someone. This is actually fair, from a Rawlsian point of view, according to my casino argument.

We must also remember Nozick's observation that to say that one's talents to make money are merely good luck, and not a result of free will or hard work, is a difficult thing to say–think for example of all the practice that someone must do to play the piano well, even if born with natural talent.

Earlier in this book I explained the theory of the upward spiral and why, if XYAB economics is adopted, it increases prosperity in an economy, and if enough net new wealth is created this could, eventually, end poverty and lift everyone up into prosperity. I believe this. But if it were to happen, it would not be soon, it could take 1000 years (and it is really plausible only when one compares the poor today with the poor 1000 years earlier) and there would be tough, significant struggles along the long road ahead. What I have said now, that we must favor XYAB even in a world of scarce resources, should maintain a healthy economics until we can solve the problem of poverty once and for all.

So, in this book, I have explained the XYAB theory of economics, making money, stealing money, and how an economy can achieve prosperity.

From the Author

I hope you enjoyed reading this. If you liked this book, won't you please tell a friend about it, or write a review of it online? Thanks!

Also please be sure to take a look at my other books:

Fiction:

The Golden Wand Trilogy

The Prince, The Girl, and the Revolution

Rob Seablue and the Eye of Tantalus

Project Utopia

The Office of Heavenly Restitution

Nonfiction:

The Apple of Knowledge

Golden Rule Libertarianism

What They Won't Tell You About Objectivism

About the Author

At the age of fifteen, Russell Hasan read "Atlas Shrugged" and decided that he wanted to become a philosopher and novelist when he grew up. Since then, he has written several books, with a focus on fantasy and science fiction, libertarian politics, and philosophical epistemology.

He majored in philosophy at Vassar, holds a law degree from the University of Connecticut, and at different points in his life has worked as a lawyer and as a software engineer. His distinctions include having written for the famous libertarian magazine Liberty for several years, and having read over three hundred fantasy and science fiction novels during his lifetime.

He lives in the United States, and is an obsessive New York Yankees fan.

Copyright Details

XYAB Economics copyright 2017 by Russell Hasan

All rights reserved. Published by Russell Hasan. Except as permitted under U.S. copyright law, no part of this publication in whole or in part may be copied, downloaded, uploaded, distributed, transmitted, or reproduced, in any form and by any means now known or later invented, whether electronic, mechanical, recording, photocopying, or otherwise, nor may this publication or any part thereof be stored in a database or information storage and retrieval system, without the prior express written consent and permission of the publisher.

Russell Hasan

Norwalk CT USA

russellhasan.com

This book first published by Russell Hasan in August, 2017

Made in the USA
Middletown, DE
08 November 2017